To Jean
Best wishes
David

(MAY 2011)

CW00838722

Rebecca
Our Wonderful Gift

David Jones

authorHOUSE®

AuthorHouse™ UK Ltd.
500 Avebury Boulevard
Central Milton Keynes, MK9 2BE
www.authorhouse.co.uk
Phone: 08001974150

First published by AuthorHouse 12/15/2010

ISBN: 978-1-4520-9918-7 (sc)
ISBN: 978-1-4567-7053-2 (dj)

THANK YOU

To Sue and Nick Pye for the countless hours they spent with me in what
at times was a very emotional journey during the writing of this book.
To all the other contributors for their own insight of Rebecca.
And to Rebecca, herself, an inspirational young lady
whose enjoyment of life was an example to us all.

Chapter One

Our Wonderful Gift

IT had been a journey into the unknown. A journey that had taken four years.

During that time the young couple had endured a rollercoaster of emotions, frustrations and challenges, but they remained fervently optimistic that their patience would ultimately be rewarded.

And it had.

Journey's end was in sight - just 10 miles to go - and the thrill of it all showed upon their faces.

Sue and Nick Pye could not have been happier on that crisp December morning in 1995 as they set off for Kirkby, a suburb of Liverpool, knowing that this was the day their lives were going to change forever.

But panic set in. They were close to their destination, but not knowing the area so well had become lost. In their haste to arrive on time they had forgotten the map they had been given and the phone number that was on it and their anxiety over being late for their appointment increased.

Sue's heart was beating faster than she had ever experienced. "I was sitting in the car saying to myself 'they'll think we don't want her,'" she said, as her husband frantically tried to locate the address. But fortunately a postman came to their rescue and they were soon driving into the small close and parking outside a semi-detached house.

The previous 24 hours had brought them the news they had yearned, and with it the sense of excitement and expectation, in addition to some apprehension. Now, though, the moment had arrived. They were going to see their daughter for the first time.

After all the uncertainty the couple had endured they had finally been accepted as adoptive parents, and as they knocked on the door of foster mum Paula's house they were just moments away from seeing the baby who would make their family complete.

When the door opened their faces revealed the unease of arriving later than arranged, but they were immediately put at ease by their Family Placement Officer, who greeted them and explained that she, too, had had difficulty finding the address.

Nick and Sue were shown into the cosy lounge and their eyes immediately focussed on the little bundle being held by the foster mum.

"Walking into Paula's home was the most nerve-wracking thing that I have ever done," said Sue. "All I could see was her face. She was wide awake and she had a huge grin. My immediate reaction was 'she's going to be ours. I can't believe this'. I remember Nick filling up and not saying a huge amount, but he was the first one to hold her.

"I didn't want to hold her," Sue admitted. "I was scared; absolutely petrified. I was not worried about dropping her, it was more like 'would she like me? How was I going to bond with this total stranger?'

"After waiting so long to actually become a mum, to become one in a day with literally less than 24 hours notice was scary, compared to the fact that most mums had nine months to prepare and usually are still not completely ready.

"She sat on Nick's knee and I sat next to her. I know it is a cliché but it was love at first sight and I absolutely adored her from that moment. She had smiling eyes, a really cheeky grin and red, rosy cheeks. She was gorgeous."

The new parents had chosen to call their little daughter Rebecca, but decided to retain her birth name of Lyndsey as her middle name.

Rebecca had been born on June 30th, 1995, and had weighed 2.04kg. She had spent a short period in Fazakerley Hospital but had been looked after since mid-July by her foster mum.

Rebecca, who wore a light blue dress with white cardigan and white tights, lay contented while Nick and Sue learned as much as they could about her from Paula. She explained that the six month old, quite a chubby little thing now, was feeding well from the bottle and was an extremely placid baby.

It was obvious from the way she spoke how attached Paula had become to the child, and the love she had for her, but she knew eventually that she would have to give her up. She had been a foster mum to a number of children, mainly babies, but Rebecca, she said, had been her favourite.

Sue and Nick posed for photographs with their baby, completed some official paperwork, sought further information from Paula and importantly got more acquainted with their daughter. There were further photos, too.

"It all seemed unreal," commented Nick. "You had to pinch yourself that it was actually happening. She was so happy, contented and just absolutely adorable. It was really quite something to hold her; a wholly new experience."

Those first two hours of contact with her was like a dream fulfilled. The frustrations the couple had faced during a long, drawn out adoption process, were now a distant memory. No longer the heartache of whether they would ever have a child. The lovely little girl being cradled by the foster mum was theirs. It was the happiest moment of their lives and they could look forward to bringing the baby up as their own. Life could not be sweeter.

Yet there was still one hurdle to overcome, due to the Christmas holidays being imminent. Rebecca's official 'handover' could not take place until January 2nd. It was anything but ideal, yet after waiting so long for a child Sue and Nick knew another week or so was not going to make a great deal of difference, especially as Paula was happy for the new parents to visit Rebecca each day over the holiday.

Finally, it was time for reluctant farewells, but arrangements were made for the couple to return the next day.

Their prayers answered, Sue and Nick were almost totally oblivious of the journey home to Childwall as they chatted excitedly about meeting Rebecca, and all the plans that had to be made for her eventual homecoming. Yet, despite their deliriously happy mood and sense of wonderment over what the future would hold for their new family, Nick's decision to return to work that day in his Liverpool city centre solicitors' office brought them back down to earth.

However, in the Pye household at least, Christmas had come early with the greatest present they could have wished for.

"It really was amazing," said Sue. "We had gone back to the foster mum's the next day to see Rebecca and she asked us if we would like to take her home for a few hours to meet the grandparents. We would have jumped at the chance but it wasn't possible because we didn't have a baby seat for the car. Paula didn't drive, so she didn't have one, either, so I rang my brother, whose youngest was then two, and thankfully they still had theirs. So the following day we took Rebecca to her new home."

It was an extra special Christmas Eve, too. Sue and Nick had invited friends round long before they knew about the "arrival" of Rebecca, and not surprisingly she became the centre of attention at the party, before they had to return her to the foster mum's in Kirkby in the early evening. But they knew they would be making the same journey again in less than 24 hours as arrangements had been made for Rebecca to spend Christmas Day with them.

The happy couple then attended the traditional Christingle service at Allerton United Reformed Church, where they were members. News of the new addition to their family had become widespread, and they were surrounded by church friends wanting to hear more about their baby.

When Christmas Day dawned Sue was concerned about the weather and driving conditions. "When we woke up it was very icy and we had to get to Kirkby. Our road was on a hill and the car literally slid down it, and I was thinking we would never see Rebecca again because we were going to go through the railings at the bottom of the hill."

The previous few days had been hectic, to say the least, with little time to shop for the necessities a little baby required. So it was with reluctance that the couple had to turn down the chance of keeping Rebecca at home on Christmas night because they didn't have a cot, any baby clothes - and only one pack of nappies!

They negotiated the drive to Kirkby safely, picked Rebecca up, and then headed to church for the Christmas morning service.

Said Sue: "I remember getting into church and one of our friends, David

Jones, who was on duty that morning, was the first to see Rebecca. We crept in at the back as the first hymn was being sung, and I remember Malcolm, our minister, coming down the aisle and asking 'can I tell everybody?' and we said 'yes, of course you can.'

"He returned to the front of the church as the hymn was ending and extended a special welcome to us and, more especially, to the new addition to the family. There was an absolute silence for a split second and then everyone applauded. It was just wonderful. Probably, there might have been a tear in my eye then."

Thoughts of an early departure after the service to take Rebecca home, settle her down and prepare for the rest of what was going to be a frantic Christmas day were dashed as the couple were effectively mobbed by the large congregation.

"As you can imagine, it took quite a while getting out of church that morning," Sue continued. "Everyone wanted to see Rebecca. The church had been full and well wishers surrounded us. I was given a large bunch of chrysanthemums with large pompom blooms and was asked to give them to Paula from the church with their love and thanks - the love and thanks for Rebecca."

Not unnaturally, there was only one focus for the rest of the day in the Pye home, where things didn't run quite as smoothly as planned.

"I totally ruined the Christmas lunch because Rebecca was crying and I didn't know what to do with her," Sue admitted. "Nick was running round saying 'what do we do?', and we were also trying to entertain an elderly lady from church, who came for Christmas lunch, and my step aunt. We tried to be as normal as we could, which was very hard. Mum and dad came round later in the day and lots of photographs were taken.

"Somebody had bought Rebecca a dress and as soon as we came home from church I changed her into it because I wanted her in something that belonged to her from someone in the family. But we changed her back again later because we didn't want to upset the foster mum. She had come beautifully dressed, but I felt I wanted her in those clothes."

Journeys back and forth to Kirkby continued to be frequent, with detours for shopping expeditions a necessity.

"Before we picked her up each day we would visit town as soon as the shops were open," said Sue. "I think the people in Mothercare must have thought we were totally mad. People normally buy a pram and ask the shop to keep it or deliver it in a couple of months time, but we wanted to take it there and then. We needed it, although the shop assistants must have looked at me and thought I wasn't very pregnant!

"Then January 2nd came. We hadn't slept the night before because this was it, Rebecca was coming home to stay this time and were weren't having to hand her back. That was a big step.

"Nick took the day off, which was unusual, and we went and collected her. We said our goodbyes to Paula, vowed to keep in touch, and we brought our baby home.

"Then it was a case of 'what do we do now?' We had our daughter, and it was scary, very scary. We still had lots of people coming to visit but we had to do the practical things, too, like register her with our GP and organise family allowance. We had to complete paperwork because it was a different situation from when you have a birth child, and then Nick went down into Liverpool to obtain a temporary birth certificate.

"We had daily calls, too, from the health visitor but it did take us a few weeks to get settled into a routine with Rebecca."

It was seven years earlier, in September 1988, that the couple had married at Allerton, just a year after their engagement while on holiday on the Greek island of Rhodes.

Sue, the youngest of three, was born in Liverpool's Oxford Street Maternity Hospital on July 16, 1965. She has two brothers, Don and Dave. Nick, also Liverpool-born on March 10, 1958, has a sister, Jacqui.

Coincidentally, Nick and Don had been best friends since primary school days, and Sue's first recollections of her future husband was at Sunday School when Nick used to chase the seven-year-old down the corridor pulling her pigtails.

The friendship continued as they grew up, mainly through social activities involving Nick and her brother. When Sue was old enough she joined them and other friends at the pub on a Sunday evening, plucking up the courage to invite him to a work's night out one Christmas. But there was disappointment as he had already made plans, so she took her brother, Don, instead.

However, from the moment Nick invited her to a young solicitors' event the following February, the relationship started to blossom. Sue was 18 at the time, seven years his junior, but she already knew that he was the one with whom she wanted to spend the rest of her life.

After their wedding five years later, the happy couple settled into married life in Childwall, just round the corner from her parents' home. Both had full time jobs. Nick, who went to Liverpool University and Law College in Chester, had been made a partner at the Liverpool firm of solicitors, Cuff Roberts, a year before, while his wife worked for Littlewoods Index, the catalogue shop, as a supervisor.

Like all newlyweds they had discussed the possibility of starting a family, as they wanted children to be very much part of their lives, but they decided against making firm plans for at least a year. Life still remained hectic, both at work and socially, and they also worked hard to get their new home in south Liverpool as they wanted it.

A year past, then another, but there were still no signs of Sue becoming pregnant. They sought medical advice, resulting in a series of tests to determine what, if anything, was wrong. The conclusion was not what the couple wanted to hear - it was unlikely they could have children naturally.

IVF treatment was considered, but ultimately they decided that if they couldn't have a child of their own they would look to adopt. Little did they know, however, that the adoption process was an arduous one, requiring incredible patience, and that it would be years before they discovered whether their application to adopt a child would be approved.

Sue explained: "We put our names down in 1990 and waited and waited. The list for those people wishing to adopt, we were told, was extremely long so we just carried on our lives as a young married couple doing all the things young married couples do, like working, going on holidays and getting the house straight.

"I used to ring up the adoption agency (Liverpool City Council) to find out how far we were up the list. Apparently, they used to take seven or eight people each year, and I think we waited nearly four years to get to the top of the list."

Slow though the process was, and the fact that the couple knew the complications of a proposed adoption, they remained optimistic.

"There wasn't that much red tape, but quite a few hurdles, which we had expected. They asked about our childhoods, families and friends, and what we thought we would bring to an adoption and how we would cope with it.

"Those were the sort of questions I don't know how anybody could actually answer because you don't know what your reaction would be. You don't know how you'll cope. You hope you'll cope well, but like any other parent who has got a natural child you don't know until it actually happens.

"I think we are both fairly level headed people so we tried not to let it bother us," continued Sue. "There were times when some of the questions we were asked seemed trivial and I didn't see where they were going. We had separate interviews and a report was written about us, and then read back to us. The interviews were easy to handle because I was prepared to do anything. If they had told me to jump through hoops backwards and naked I would have done.

"I think Nick found it harder because his training had taught him to analyse such questions, but we kept an open mind about those. We just thought there would be an end product, and the end product was what we wanted, so we had to do what we had to do.

"We had been asked whether we would take a disabled child and we had declined. We felt we had waited so long, and with the disappointment that we couldn't have our own children we didn't know whether we could cope with a disabled child. We didn't think that that was what we were cut out for, but we didn't mind whether the child was a boy or girl. We also wondered if they would try to place a baby with us who had certain similarities, but we were told the main condition was meeting the child's needs.

"We were also informed that there were always two couples who were considered by the Adoption Panel for approval for the one child, so they wouldn't just be presenting our case to the Panel suggesting we were the right parents for a specific child.

"It was around November 1994 when we finally received a letter to say they were ready to take up our application if we still wanted to go ahead with adoption. In the January, we went on a course for three Saturdays which involved group meetings and role play, and some people gave us their accounts about how adoption had either been successful for them or not.

"The following month we had our first meeting with what they classed a Family Placement Officer. She came and spoke to us in some detail. We then had to have police checks and medicals, more interviews, and we also had to give them names of two referees who would speak on our behalf."

Finally, their application went in front of the Adoption Panel, and in June 1995 they received confirmation that they had been approved as prospective adopters for a child up to two years old.

The dream of becoming parents had taken a significant step forward and with Sue desperate to become a mum she hoped then the process would be speeded up.

"We tried to get on as normally as we possibly could," Sue went on. "I suppose there was that anticipation as to whether there would be a phone call or a letter through the door. I was buying little bits and putting them away, but we hadn't told anybody. It wasn't public knowledge that we were going through the adoption process because we didn't want to tell anyone in case it didn't work. We eventually told my parents and Nick's father, but not in great detail because we felt it was very personal and we wanted the element of surprise, really.

"We knew nothing from the June until December 21st. It had been my day off and I had taken my mum to Southport. It had been our little thing that in December before Christmas we would go there and do some shopping and have lunch.

"On our return, I dropped my mum off and I went home to find a hand delivered letter pushed through the door. It was from the Family Placement Officer asking me to ring her at home. I immediately rang her and she asked if she could come round.

"I actually made some mince pies while I waited for her. Later, I wondered why I had made them when I knew exactly what she was going to tell me. It was a strange feeling. I was actually very calm about it outwardly, but inwardly I was probably a total and utter mess because I was wondering whether she was going to tell us we have a child or say that all of a sudden they were not going to have us as parents.

"But I had this feeling she was going to tell us something exciting - and it was! She arrived and said that we had been placed with a little girl of five and a half months old who was with foster parents and we could visit her the following day.

"She asked me what I thought of the news and I just replied 'it is wonderful'. I think she was shocked by my reaction but I was just trying to keep calm. I am not the sort of person to show a huge amount of emotion, at least not in public. She also asked me if I was going to phone Nick with the news. I said 'oh yes', but I was waiting for her to go before I phoned him. She didn't, so rather than use the phone near where I was sitting, I went out into the hall and used the one there.

"It must have been about five o'clock. He answered in a rather brusque manner and I said I hoped I was not disturbing him. He replied 'it's alright, what is it?' and I said I wanted to let him know that he was now a daddy. There was a silence at the other end of the phone, and then he said 'I'll ring you back'."

The Family Placement Officer gave Sue details about where the foster mum lived and said she would see them both at the address in Kirkby at 10 o'clock the next morning. Then she left.

A few minutes later, Nick rang back. "He didn't say a huge amount," said Sue. "He just wanted a few details, really. He was very quiet and you could tell he had obviously been crying, but with joy, and he had gone out into the corridor to see if there was anyone he could share the news with. Luckily, his partner who had given us a reference was still in her office so he went and told her. She was delighted. He also told another partner and I felt very miffed about that because I hadn't told anyone. I was still trying to keep it a secret. He said he would finish a few things off at the office and he would see me at my brothers, where I was babysitting. Surprisingly, I hadn't shed any tears over our wonderful news."

The call from Sue had taken Nick by surprise. "It was all very sudden, really," he admitted. "I told a couple of close friends at work and we had a little laugh and cry about it. I am accused of being over zealous about work and I tried to pass on a couple of things that needed to be done the next morning. But I was basically shoved out of the door and told those sort of things would take care of themselves and it was a matter of what was important to us."

Sue's first priority was to go out to the general store at the top of the road and buy Christmas cards - from their new daughter to the grandparents. Her brother, Don, and wife Delyth were going out to a Christmas concert at the Philharmonic Hall, so Sue then drove to their house to look after her nieces.

So far, apart from her husband, Sue hadn't told anyone about the happenings of the past few hours, but was desperately keen to share her joy with others.

"I wanted it to be that Nick and I told everyone together. My mum and dad were at home and I wanted to tell them, but I didn't want to tell them our news without Nick being there.

"Two of my nieces had gone to bed but Catherine, the eldest, who was six, was sitting there with me. I said to her, 'can you keep a secret?' and I told her she was going to get a little cousin. Then I sent here to bed so she couldn't tell her mum and dad.

"Nick eventually arrived from work and so I then rang my mum and dad, Barbara and Gordon, and asked them to come round to my brother's because we needed to speak to them. On arrival, we just handed them the card I had bought which said 'Happy Christmas, Gran and Granddad'. They were absolutely delighted. There were a few tears from my mother, as usual, and then Don and Delyth arrived home so we told them, too.

"Then we went off to see Nick's father, Geoffrey. It must have been about 11 o'clock and I think he wondered what we were doing there at that time. We handed him the Christmas card from Rebecca and he got very emotional. He was thrilled because it was going to be his first grandchild. We returned home and I rang my other brother and Nick rang his sister. Despite wishing to tell so many more people, we thought it was getting a little late and we didn't think people would appreciate us ringing them after midnight."

Not unnaturally, sleep didn't come easily for either of them that night, as they talked about the day's momentous events. Discussion also turned to other important aspects of parenthood - considering names, which was appropriate at the time, where they would have to shop for baby clothes and how they would decorate the nursery. Christmas shopping, they knew, was frantic enough, but the fact that they had so little time to buy the necessities for a baby with stores closing for Christmas was added pressure.

"It wasn't like now with 24 hour shopping," stated Sue. "The internet wasn't up and running. We had no pram, no cot, no car seat - they were just some of the thoughts rushing through our heads. We'd hardly had any sleep so it was no wonder I woke the following morning and was sick through nerves. I couldn't manage breakfast. Nerves had got the better of me at that point, and the fact that Nick informed me that he would have to go to the office to hand in an important file before we journeyed to Kirkby to meet our baby for the first time didn't help."

However, it was a Christmas to remember for them both, as they became acquainted with their lovely daughter, showing her off to the proud grandparents, the rest of the family and friends.

Yes, there were still anxieties over the responsibilities of looking after a baby for the first time, but it was also a time of fulfilment and enjoyment.

Sue admitted: "The only experience I had was looking after my nieces occasionally. However prepared you are mentally, I don't think you are physically prepared for a child. I think you can read all the books under the sun and be told all the things you think you need to be told, but nothing actually prepares you.

"We just got on with it. It was a case of we've got her now and we have to cope, so let's just do it as best as we possibly can. We took advice from people, we listened to people, and then did it our own way as everyone does.

"We just loved her, basically, and hoped the love we gave her would be enough."

The Pyes were now a complete family unit. Mum and dad had the child they had longed for, a gorgeous fair-haired daughter with a radiant smile. Rebecca had a wonderful home with devoted parents whose wish was for her to grow up in a loving environment, happy and contented.

And that was the case.

Sue and Nick watched as their daughter flourished over the next few years, a little girl who captivated the hearts and minds of everyone with whom she came into contact.

So when Rebecca became seriously ill no-one could have been prepared for the shattering news which was to follow - a dramatic turn of events that left Sue and Nick devastated, their world turned upside down, as their precious little girl was left fighting for her life.

Chapter Two

The Happy Early Years

LIFE changes with the arrival of a little one.

It is not just the child that has to adapt, either. The parents, having experienced married life and the love for each other that develops with it, are suddenly thrust into a new situation that brings additional demands, far greater responsibility and the need for flexibility.

There is also the important aspect of bonding with your child. That begins at birth normally when the mother and baby immediately strike up a rapport. It is a special relationship of love and affection that lasts a lifetime.

In Sue and Nick's case it was different. Adoption meant that they didn't have that immediate intimacy, so the first few weeks after taking Rebecca home were important in helping the six month old to become accustomed to new surroundings in a new home with a new mum and dad.

Being with Rebecca almost every minute of every day allowed Sue to quickly develop a special bond. For Nick, though, the transformation to parenthood was never going to be as easy, given his demanding job and the long hours he spent at work.

"I used to worry about how I would take to being a daddy," he admitted. "But from that first Saturday when Rebecca came to our house and I held her and she went to sleep and there was this lovely bundle of warmth in my arms, I knew she was ours.

"Sue's mum and dad and my father came over, and my aunt, who had been away with her family in Newcastle, arrived in the evening. I remember her saying to Rebecca 'you lucky, lucky child.' But I thought it was us who were lucky."

Nick, who began at Cuff Roberts in 1980 as an articled clerk, had a work pattern that comprised early starts and late finishes, but the arrival of Rebecca called for changes, at least initially.

Said Nick: "Because of the sort of work I did which involved working long hours I was anxious that I should try and do what I could to be at home more. It meant curtailing working extra hours at weekends to join in the joy of being with Rebecca and being at gatherings with other members of the family when she was the centre of attention."

Her fair hair and blue eyes gave Rebecca a similar colouring to Nick's, and the similarities provided a source of amusement.

"It was uncanny because people who didn't know the circumstances said how alike we were and there was no mistaking who her father was, and that was something that was said more and more.

"There may be something in a father and daughter relationship because while she had her own sense of humour, it was perhaps something like mine. But she was happy, very loving, wanted to be with people and didn't often cry. She became part of the family quite easily.

"It is accepted that it is far easier for adoption to happen when you are dealing with a baby. It is a different kettle of fish if you are seeking to adopt an older child. Fortunately, we didn't have to deal with some of the anxieties an older child would have brought because they would have been more aware of their surroundings.

"The weekends were invaluable for us just being together, doing things together, like pushing the pram when we were out walking. It was wonderful to be what we would perceive now to be a complete family unit. We used to have lunch at my aunt's on a Saturday and see Sue's mum and dad later, and my father on a Sunday. Sue's parents were particularly good because when I couldn't be about during the week they were always there to do what they could to support Sue which was tremendous.

"We had had a happy married life but we had always known that there was one other thing that was needed to make things complete and that was for a child to be in our lives. Emotionally, being a dad just evolved, but when it came to practicalities Sue took over. I was the one who prepared bottles and dealt with the hygiene aspects, but it was Sue who did the hard work. Rebecca just adapted.

"It was a new life for us. We had been told life would be different and we were thrust into it more quickly perhaps than in a situation where a child is conceived naturally, because there is a little bit of time to think and plan. We didn't have that time because when the wheels started to move and we were told there was a potential placement it was like a rollercoaster. From within a fortnight of living the life we had become used to, to becoming a family of three was quite a change."

Nevertheless, Nick continued to juggle a busy work schedule, with family commitments and a hectic social life that brought additional demands.

"I tried to get home as quickly as possible from work, as any father would, but I tried to retain those activities that we had become involved in, and the responsibilities they entailed," he said.

"On one occasion, we took Rebecca to a church meeting which was probably a daft thing to do, but everyone thought it was amusing. Sue gave up things like being a manager at church, but one of my failings was that I continued to be involved in certain things that, in hindsight, I should have stopped. At church, I was secretary to the committee of Managers, and we had both been established members of the dramatic society. Sue stopped going immediately and I didn't participate but continued to be treasurer. I also had a season ticket for Liverpool and we used to joke quite a lot that I should stop going, but I managed to resist that!"

Sue had decided prior to Christmas that with Rebecca's imminent arrival in the new year she would have to finish working. She had switched jobs from a city centre store to a local opticians, situated at the shops close to where she lived. They had been unaware that she and her husband had been going through the adoption process.

"I was working four days a week and I had rung and left a message on the answer phone because I was supposed to be at work on the day we saw Rebecca for the first time. I went in to see the boss after we had visited

Rebecca and explained the situation. He was delighted for me because he had had a little boy six months earlier and he knew how wonderful it was. I told him I wouldn't be back before Christmas obviously, and I needed to speak to him afterwards. But I knew in my heart of hearts that there was no way I was going back to work. I didn't want to. I had my work cut out and a new job looking after Rebecca."

Those early days at home with her daughter proved priceless as Sue settled into the role she had longed for.

"We struck up a lovely relationship within a few days. We were there together 24 seven and Rebecca very quickly came to realise that it would be me who was there for her. I adored her smile and her giggle. She had a very dirty laugh, really, a sort of chuckle. Her eyes always lit up when she smiled and she always seemed to be happy, apart from when she was poorly with the snuffles or was chesty, and then she was a bit grouchy.

"Sleep patterns were sorted out fairly quickly. She slept in our bedroom for two months so we could get to know her better. But very quickly she went into her own room.

"When she came to us she was just starting to be weaned. That was slightly difficult because she did enjoy her bottle. We worked out that we had to hide it until food had been administered because if she saw the bottle she wouldn't want anything else. By the time she was nine months old she was sitting in her highchair at breakfast enjoying cereal and a round of toast.

"Being her mum became second nature. I just seemed to enjoy her so much. I wanted to be there with her all the time. Her personality made her adapt so easily. As long as she felt secure she was happy."

But help, if any were needed, was never far away and both Sue and Nick were grateful for the support from family and friends.

"My parents, being grandparents already, were delighted to have another granddaughter. They were there if we needed them but they weren't round every five minutes. I used to put Rebecca in the pram, walk round and have a cup of tea with them and mum and dad would have a cuddle and take care of Rebecca for an hour or so. Mum would also give me a hand with the housework if I needed it. We just got on like that, really. They couldn't do enough for her, as with all their grandchildren.

"We received quite a lot of support from friends and Nick's work colleagues were very good, too, letting him pop home at lunch times to see if everything was okay. But we didn't get any help from Social Services because we didn't really need any. We could have phoned them if there were any problems, but there weren't any, so we did what any new parents do and just muddled through."

As Rebecca approached the milestone of her first birthday, the family decided to take a holiday in the Isle of Man. Originally, Nick thought he had won a family trip to the island, but the prize was for a single passenger on foot on a Manx ferryboat. However, they took the car over with them and, despite some miserable weather, had a fantastic time.

"I remember the boat trip," recalled Sue. "It was a really bad crossing and Nick and I were not very well. We kept passing Rebecca to one another as one of us ran off to the toilet to be sick, but Rebecca just sat and giggled for the full four hours we were on the boat. She wasn't affected at all by the rolling of the boat, but Nick and I were as green as anything.

"It was the first time in a hotel with Rebecca. We had taken a travel cot and she slept at the bottom of our bed. They didn't have a bath in the room we were given so trying to wash an 11 month old child in a shower wasn't the easiest thing to do. It was a slippery, rather wet bathing time, as one of us held her and the other showered her in a tiny cubicle."

The beach was an obvious lure and they watched their daughter playing in the sand for the first time. "Nick bought Rebecca the most enormous bucket and spade, nearly as big as her," said Sue, "and we couldn't turn it over when it was full of sand - it was that heavy!"

There was plenty of excitement as Rebecca celebrated her first birthday - but it was also tinged with sadness.

The day coincided with the church's minister, the Rev Malcolm Shapland, who had welcomed the family on that Christmas morning, leaving to take up another post. He was a popular man, respected by everyone, and the farewells to him on the Sunday morning left Sue and Nick, as well as many others, feeling low. However, their daughter's party in the afternoon proved the perfect antidote.

Rebecca fell asleep on the way home and was completely oblivious to the preparations being made by her mum and dad for the family and friends who had been invited to share in the joy of her birthday. Her infectious smile that captivated the hearts of so many was again in evidence during the afternoon and helped to cheer everyone up.

"We had bought her a slide and my mum and dad had bought her a swing," Sue recalled. "We went into the garden and she had a play on the swing. Afterwards, her other granddad - who became known as granddad Geoff to Rebecca - offered to hold her for a while, but no sooner had he taken her than she was sick all down him.

"I had made a three-tiered birthday cake with little teddies all over it," Sue continued. "Everybody just had a pleasant afternoon and Rebecca thoroughly enjoyed it. Plenty of photographs were taken and, while Rebecca had little idea what was going on, it was something we had looked forward to do, celebrating birthdays with her, and this was her first one."

Those first six months had been a thoroughly fulfilling, rewarding and exciting time in the Pye household as Rebecca developed her own little character, but she was not officially their daughter until their application to the court for the Adoption Order was granted. The couple had applied in the Spring, but with certain procedures, checks and safeguards to be undertaken, and to ensure that what was proposed would be in Rebecca's best interests, the process was laborious.

"It was a little bit unsettling even though it was a quite straightforward process as we were told that there was no likelihood of any party objecting to us legally adopting her," stated Nick. "But until the adoption actually happened and the order made she wasn't officially ours. Happily, though, we were advised that a hearing had been set for Friday, August 16, at Liverpool County Court. It was a private hearing with a judge dressed in civilian clothes, rather than court attire. We met the social worker and a little bit of evidence was given to state the facts and the adoption order was made. We were invited into the judge's chambers to have a photograph taken with him. It was a memento and something we could talk about to Rebecca in years to come about the day when she legally became ours.

"It was seen as a happy event in family courts, where there were lots of unhappy things going on, and it was a really good feeling for us. A solicitor from our office had been with us and had appeared on our behalf, and then we all went off and had coffee and cakes at a local restaurant."

The couple were eager to have Rebecca baptised but it could not be contemplated until that momentous day in court. But with the issue resolved plans were made for another important landmark in her young life on Sunday, November 24, 1996.

"We wanted it to be a celebration of a really happy and wonderful thing that had happened to all of us," said Nick. "We had made a point of asking a lot of people who had been very kind to us, including the foster mum, so everybody important in Rebecca's life was there and the church was packed. The Rev Sandra Dears, who had got to know us and Rebecca quite well, took the service and baptised her."

Rebecca was too big for a christening gown but looked lovely in a little navy blue cardigan and skirt, both edged with tartan, with black patent leather shoes with a tartan bow. Because it was winter she also wore a smock wool coat in navy blue with a navy blue beret with a little bow.

The family had chosen all the hymns for the service, including a favourite selected by one particular aunt. It was called 'Tell out my soul, the greatness of the Lord'. "That expressed how life had become complete and perhaps how good things were for us and a reason to be thankful," said Nick.

One of the biggest problems had been in deciding who would act as godparents and in the end seven were chosen!

Said Sue: "The whole service revolved around Rebecca, which was lovely. It was extra special because the members of the church were there for one purpose - to be there for Rebecca and us."

A reception followed at the nearby police social club attended by 100 people and Rebecca, true to form, slept through most of it. But it was Sue and Nick's way of saying thank you to the many people for helping them along the way.

Rebecca had cut her first tooth on January 4, 1996, just two days after moving into her new home, but by the end of that year there were few signs of her talking and walking, although without comparisons to draw on it was difficult to measure her progress and to assess whether she was achieving her potential. It was of some concern to Sue that when she did eventually start talking her speech was difficult to understand, but once she began walking at the age of two there was no stopping her.

"We were just happy she was getting along, doing things at her pace and enjoying life," said Sue. "If you look at all the books people say that their children started walking at around 10 months. Rebecca didn't, but the health visitor told us not to worry.

"No-one mentioned her speech, either. We understood it and maybe if we had again had someone to compare with we might have thought she was not doing as well. But when she went through her yearly assessments with the health visitor they were happy."

The first indication of any health problems came when Rebecca was two and a half. At that time, Sue and Nick were in the process of trying to sell their house, and Rebecca became violently sick all of a sudden.

"I noticed that her eye had turned out. It returned again to normal, but I took her to the doctors and they referred us to the hospital," stated Sue. "They had a look at her eyes but they were not concerned. They said she probably had a turn in her eye and I should not worry about it. However, I did notice that when she was tired her eye would wander, but it wasn't of any great concern because it was something we thought that lots of children suffered from. We knew it could be corrected by either wearing glasses or by surgery.

"But Rebecca was fantastic, fun-loving and always very sociable. She did mischievous things but nothing out of the ordinary.

"She was certainly a daddy's girl. When daddy wasn't about mummy would do, but as soon as daddy came home it was different. Daddy was soft with her and mummy was the hard one who said 'no'."

Sue and Nick agreed that they would put Rebecca's name down to attend Childwall Church of England School. "She was only two at the time, which was far too early, but I put it down anyway," said Sue. "My brothers and I had been to Childwall and I felt it was the right place for Rebecca as it was a small school and very friendly, and it also had the Christian ethos which we had been brought up with."

House moves can have unsettling effects, particularly for children, but when the family moved just over half a mile to a semi detached property in Childwall Park Avenue only the parents felt the strain.

"The move did not affect Rebecca in any way whatsoever," Sue remarked. "It was July 3, 1998, and she went to my mum and dad's while we moved in. They brought her round early evening and I said to her 'this is your bedroom now'. Rebecca said 'okay' and that was the end of it. She had a look round the house and settled into it straight away, not questioning the fact that she was never going back to her other house. As far as she was concerned this was home now and she was happy."

Rebecca was three when she started to go to the Bluebell Nursery a couple of mornings a week. This increased to four times a week as she approached school age and her mum found very quickly how much she missed her around the house.

"There was never an 'I don't want to go' situation," said Sue. "I was a bit upset about her leaving me, but she wasn't. It was nice that when she came out she was really pleased to see me. We went home and had lunch and I would try to find out what she had been doing at nursery, but I rarely got anything out of her. They always had summer and Christmas concerts and she was always involved in those."

Rebecca attended other groups, too, which saw her mixing much more with children of her own age. And it was as a result of these that Sue became aware that perhaps her daughter was not making the progress she should have been.

"We went to Pram Club at the local church, All Saints in Childwall, and Tots and Co at our own church, so she had quite a busy social life," Sue went on. "She also started Tumble Tots, a national gymnastics club for youngsters, and there I did start noticing her co-ordination was very poor. She couldn't go along the ladder with one hand in front of the other like other children. It was only little things like that and I put them to the back of my mind thinking that there are a lot of people who don't co-ordinate very well. But she could do other things so I was not worried about it.

"Rebecca wasn't very good at reading and writing, either. She enjoyed being read to, but very rarely did she want to colour pictures in. She would just scribble.

"I thought she was just shy, but she probably found it difficult to mix with others. A few times when we had gone out with other children of similar age, Rebecca tended to stay on the sidelines and watch. Nothing was ever mentioned at the nursery. Nobody ever said she was not doing this or not doing that. I suppose the nursery was there to keep her occupied.

"Rebecca did things willingly. We never had tantrums. If I said we were going out she would go and get her coat. There was never a case of her wanting to stay in to play with toys. In fact, she didn't play with her toys very well and was not very imaginative. Where a lot of kids would have dolls or cars and play for hours with them, Rebecca was never interested in those things. The only thing she enjoyed doing was her stacking cups, which she had had from the time she came to us. She enjoyed playing with those, putting one on top of another and then knocking them down. It was like a sense of achievement to her. With her being able to do that we thought her co-ordination wasn't too bad, but I suppose after practising and practising with them, it became second nature."

One of the highlights of Rebecca's week was attending Sunday School at Allerton URC. The church was always a happy environment for her and she loved listening to the stories and taking part in the activities, including the band, where the drum was her favourite instrument. She enjoyed her roles in the nativity plays, too, and it was not uncommon to see Rebecca running round the church with her best friend, Philip Jones. Everyone at church watched her develop into a cheerful and pleasant little girl, whose smile was always a radiant feature of her jovial personality.

Holidays were another aspect of life Rebecca adored, particularly those abroad in the warm climate. She loved the water, paddling and playing on the beach, and often made herself comfortable soaking up the sun on a lounger, complete with sunglasses!

It was those family times that Nick appreciated. "Having to work long hours, you anticipate and relish the opportunity of being away together for a week or two and we had some happy trips to various places, both at home and abroad, either as a threesome or with our friends, David and Jennie."

The first day at school can be a daunting prospect for most children but Rebecca, like all the others starting at Childwall C of E at the same time in September 1999, was eased into school life, first with a week of mornings only, followed by a similar period of afternoons.

"We went on a Wednesday," said Sue, "and Rebecca's friend Philip was starting at the same time. We met Philip and his mum, Fiona, and we took photographs of the children in their new school blazers. Rebecca's hair was very long then and I had done it in pigtails for her. I remember them going in holding hands as they walked up the school yard. Rebecca wasn't worried in the least. There was no look of fear, no turning back and looking at me as if to say 'what am I doing?' She was absolutely fine.

"It was a strange feeling for me and I had this sort of fear that people would start to judge her, which nobody had done before, and I wondered how well she was going to get on. I just filled my days without her and looked forward to 3.30pm when I went to pick her up. I actually volunteered to help out in the school about half a day a week, so I had a little eye on her.

"She was not very forthcoming in telling us what she had been doing. Her stock answer was that she had sat in her coat all day and waited for me to come for her, but there was always that little glint in her eye to suggest that I didn't really know what she got up to."

Alarm bells began to ring when Sue and Nick attended a meeting with Rebecca's teacher in the October.

"She was very pleasant," said Nick, "but said that she felt Rebecca, compared to most of the others in class, was significantly less advanced and developed and was behind from an intellectual point of view, which we were quite troubled about.

"They had said she was okay at nursery without being exceptional so we didn't think there was anything unduly wrong, but we were on our guard. We thought it was probably nothing more than a problem that could be sorted educationally. We were concerned as to how she would progress and concerned whether she would be upset when she went to school for the first time, but she seemed to cope with all that so we didn't see anything at that stage other than normal progression through school life. And there was certainly no indication looking back at photographs of physical ailments. Rebecca, in fact, had been a well child and hadn't succumbed to many of the traditional childhood illnesses."

Nevertheless, the teacher's comments came as a shock, despite the fact that it was early days in their daughter's school life and it was inevitable that some children would appear to be brighter than others.

Physically she appeared as normal as the next child. Her height and weight were standard for a child of her age; her teeth had come through without problems and she had passed her latest hearing test. Yet something, somewhere, was awry - and her mum could not quite put her finger on it.

"I thought that we had to take Rebecca as she comes because we didn't know what her potential was in life," said Sue. "With me being in the school and seeing how the other children were coming on, alarm bells had started to ring very quietly. I was thinking these were either very clever kids or there was something not right with Rebecca. You don't want to hear that your child isn't as clever as the next child, but we felt she must be allowed to settle in.

"We thought she might have learning difficulties and we would be able to sort them out. We went to the doctors to get Rebecca a referral for speech therapy, but the doctor didn't seem concerned about anything else.

"She performed in the Christmas play at school and I have her on video doing that. She was just in the chorus and was singing along and keeping up with everybody."

The family, as usual, found Christmas a hectic yet happy time and, with the new Millennium fast approaching, Sue and Nick had planned a party for friends on new year's eve. Despite all the celebrations the background worries over Rebecca remained.

Before school began again Sue took Rebecca into town to buy her new shoes. Naturally, she wore them on the first morning of the new term, but it was that walk to school that highlighted a possible health issue.

"We hadn't gone as far as the end of the road when Rebecca told me she couldn't walk. I told her not to be silly, but she repeated it. We came back home and I put her in her old shoes. She did get to school, but I carried her some of the way. I was convinced the new shoes were the problem and that they would be going back to the shop. However, she wasn't able to walk home, either."

Worse was to follow. On arrival home Rebecca told her mum she couldn't remember how to go up the stairs. She managed them with help, but Sue was acutely aware that Rebecca was suffering from some kind of illness.

"I took her to the GP and he said it was probably a water infection. He took a sample and suggested we return in a week for the results. It was around mid January and Rebecca was attending dance classes at the time. We had gone to dancing after school but I could see from the way she looked there was no way she could do it. I took her back to the doctors and told him I was not happy because there was obviously something wrong with her, but

I didn't know what. The doctor told me they hadn't had the tests back and he would ring me when he got them.

"So we left it another week which, in hindsight, we shouldn't have done. We should have taken her to hospital but we didn't. I went back to the doctors and said something had to be done because she was not getting any better. I was told nothing was wrong with her and she hadn't got an infection.

"I saw a different doctor on this occasion and told her Rebecca wasn't able to walk properly, had problems getting up the stairs and was knocking into things. She asked me how long Rebecca had been breathing the way she was because she had been gasping for air. I said she had always been like that, how she had always breathed, but the doctor said she couldn't have done. I said 'sorry, that's how she had been'."

Rebecca's breathing patterns had never been an issue before so this was an unexpected assessment. The doctor appeared concerned over her general condition, alerting Sue's suspicions that whatever illness her daughter was experiencing, it was not simply a straightforward one. That was confirmed when the doctor told her hospital tests were required. Such was the urgency of the situation that an appointment was made that evening and Rebecca went in the following day for tests.

It was the beginning of February, the beginning of a nightmare and the beginning of a desperate battle for Rebecca as the medical profession, baffled at first over her symptoms, eventually came up with a diagnosis - a rare disease for which life expectancy was limited.

Life for the family was suddenly plunged into turmoil. Sue and Nick were told that in the light of their daughter's condition to prepare for the worst. She might die at any time.

The next five months proved to be a living hell.

Chapter Three

Touch And Go

THE little girl lying forlornly in the hospital bed cut a pathetic figure. Her body was covered in wires attached to monitors and tubes connected to various pieces of equipment.

It was indicative of the growing concern of medical staff for the child's condition.

Her parents sat at her bedside, the anxiety etched on their faces, looking down on their daughter, fearful of what might be wrong with her, and desperate to know whether she would make a full recovery from the illness that had plunged her into the terrible ordeal she now faced.

But answers would not come easily.

It was incredibly difficult for Sue and Nick to come to terms with recent events. Barely a few weeks before they had an apparently healthy daughter settling in to life at school and enjoying doing the things little girls did. But now here was their beloved Rebecca surrounded by nurses, doctors and machinery, fighting against some mystery illness that left her life hanging by a thread.

If there was any consolation for the parents it was the fact that the four-year-old was at least in the best place she could be to be looked after and, hopefully, make a complete recovery. Alder Hey Children's Hospital, situated in West Derby, was founded in 1914 and is one of the largest of its kind in Europe. They have over 2,000 dedicated staff treating around 200,000 children each year, from minor injuries to life-threatening conditions.

Just what Rebecca's condition was had yet to be established.

Following the worries expressed by their female GP days earlier, she was taken by her parents to an emergency clinic at the hospital. The doctor there routinely took Rebecca's blood pressure. He didn't say anything, but Sue and Nick noticed that his raised eyebrows at his findings indicated that all was not well. So he repeated the test. After receiving similar readings he told them he didn't think the equipment was working correctly and was going to get a replacement. But a third reading only confirmed the previous ones and the doctor informed them that Rebecca's blood pressure was abnormally high and dangerous. She was admitted into hospital immediately and transferred to a bed on the second floor.

During the next few days there was an urgency among the medical staff as they carried out further tests, x-rays and MRI scans to try and determine the cause of her illness. Checks were made on her kidneys, an orthopaedic team carried out bone density examinations, while staff from the neurology section were also called in and decided the youngster should be put on a steroid drip. But while so many questions remained, there were still no answers, nothing the parents could hang their hopes on that their daughter would overcome the problems that had seemingly enveloped the whole of her body.

While Sue and Nick looked for the faintest signs of an improvement they suffered a further setback when it was decided to take Rebecca by ambulance to Fazakerley Hospital for muscle tests.

"That's when we really knew how poorly she was because they were sticking needles straight into her calf muscles and she wasn't even flinching," said her mum. "She wasn't murmuring with any pain. She was just lying there letting them do it.

"Obviously, we were very concerned because we just did not know what was going on; what was happening to her. She was getting worse and worse and nobody seemed to know what was wrong. It was like walking through a minefield. We just didn't know when the next thing was going to happen to her. I think the fact that nobody was giving us any answers and nobody seemed to know anything was the hardest bit."

The days at Alder Hey for Sue were long, the nights longer. She stayed with Rebecca almost all day, every day, spending nights on a camp bed next to her daughter.

"She was far too young to leave on her own in hospital but I was not really able to sleep," she admitted. "Before we moved to ICU (Intensive Care Unit) Rebecca was in a mixed medical ward so there were all sorts of things going on and there were a lot of admissions during the night. Because I was there the nursing staff always left the medication they were giving Rebecca to me and for some unknown reason one of the doses was at 2.00 in the morning. They would wake me to tell me the tablet (for blood pressure) was there to give to Rebecca. Why it had to be in tablet form I don't know because she was unable to swallow. I had to push it right to the back of her throat to get it down. It would dissolve on the back of her tongue and she couldn't even swallow a little drink to get rid of the taste. So those sort of things I found very hard.

"In the morning I had to pack up my bed, go down to the parents' room for a shower or quick wash, and then return to the ward because I didn't want to miss the doctor's round - and you never knew when they were going to turn up. Afterwards, I sometimes had breakfast in the canteen, but quite often I didn't want to leave Rebecca, so it might be mid morning before I got a cup of tea. I didn't think about my health. At the time I was young enough to cope, although I probably went through quite a few headache tablets. It was a case of my body going on auto pilot and I just got on with it.

"At the time, we were obviously both in a state, but we were so busy trying to keep Rebecca motivated and happy as much as we possibly could, and trying to keep ourselves going in what was a very alien environment. Our feelings went on the back burner. In the first few weeks of her being in hospital I don't think we really had a chance to talk about how we were feeling. It was a case of Nick coming to the hospital and me telling him what had occurred that day and what the doctors had or hadn't said."

Naturally, there was a constant flow of family and friends to visit Rebecca, giving her mum time to have a break and freshen up. People from church and further afield kept in touch, too, anxious to let all three know they were in their thoughts and prayers.

"Rebecca would always have a smile for people when they came in," said Sue. "It was a case of 'yes, I'm still here', smile and then she would go back to sleep."

The couple remained confident Rebecca was suffering from some viral complaint from which, with the necessary medication and nursing, she would soon recover. But as parents whose job it was to comfort and care for their daughter in times of need they felt completely helpless as they watched her deteriorate. The illness was taking its toll on the youngster, both physically and mentally.

Said Sue: "When she went in to hospital she was still walking, but her ability to walk seemed to disappear over a period of three or four days because she had been struggling before that. Her cheerfulness was going, her spirit seemed to be waning and she wasn't eating or drinking, which was worrying, so they put her on a drip to give her fluids because her capacity to swallow had almost gone. Weight was just dropping off her and she was sleeping all the time. She was so weak she couldn't even get out of bed herself."

Frustration grew for the parents as test upon test was completed over the course of two weeks, but while there was some feedback from the hospital there was nothing conclusive to show from them - nothing that offered the slightest bit of encouragement to the anxious couple that they might escape from the nightmare they and Rebecca were living.

Was there just a chance that the lack of evidence from the tests suggested that it may after all be a type of virus that was attacking her system and she may recover as rapidly as the illness had developed? What hope that may have offered was dashed with the doctors' decision that Rebecca must undertake a lumber puncture without an anaesthetic to attempt to arrive at a possible diagnosis. This proved unsuccessful so it was decided that a test must be carried out under general anaesthetic, requiring a trip to the operating theatre. It became a defining moment because the operation highlighted Rebecca's deterioration.

Sue explained: "After having the lumber puncture they had great trouble getting Rebecca to breathe herself and getting her off the ventilator. I was still in the ward at the time and I was sitting there waiting for her to come back very naively thinking they would tell us to go home after a couple of days and things would get better.

"A doctor came to see me and as soon as I saw her I knew there was something wrong. Normally after theatre, the patient would come back and then the doctor would come round an hour later to see how they were doing. Rebecca hadn't come back but the doctor had. She told me the lumber puncture had gone well, but there was concern over Rebecca and they would monitor her in ICU overnight. She had been taken off the ventilator, they had got her breathing again, and I could go up to the recovery room to see her. I rang Nick, who was still at work, told him he needed to come to the hospital urgently and he said he would leave straightaway.

"I went up to the theatre and the anaesthetist spoke to me. I must have been in total shock. I showed no emotion whatsoever. But when they took me through to ICU Rebecca was sitting up in bed and didn't look too bad, so I wondered what all the fuss was about.

"Nick was still on his way and I was just standing by Rebecca's bedside when a doctor came up and said she must be vented immediately. Rebecca took hold of my hand and said 'just take me home, mummy'. Oh, how I wished I could have picked her up and run.

"To me, she looked absolutely fine, but nurses suddenly appeared round her bed and I was ushered out and the curtains were pulled round. Nick had just arrived when the head of the neurology department came up to us and told us our daughter was very ill and might not last the night. We didn't know what to do or where to go and then someone took us to the parents' room and we made a few phone calls to let my parents and Nick's father know what had happened. It was all a bit of a blur.

"After the doctor left it was a few hours before someone came and spoke to us. They told us straight that they weren't sure about Rebecca's condition, said her breathing was poor and her blood pressure so high she would be lucky to survive the night. They said they would speak to us later.

"We were both in total shock. We tried to ask what was going on but no-one was able to tell us. Whether they didn't want to tell us, or whether they didn't know what to tell us, I don't know. This had been the first indication that things were touch and go. Eventually, we got back to see

Rebecca. She had been sedated and sticky pads were all over her body to monitor her heart rate. All we could hear was the beep, beep, beep. We just sat there absolutely stunned."

There comes a point when the overwhelming nature of a situation can provoke understandable reaction; when those pent-up feelings of despair for a loved one becomes too much to bear. With their little girl so poorly, suffering from a mystery illness that was still undefined, there is no doubt that Sue and Nick were reaching that stage. Their world, so recently one of happiness and contentment, had been plunged into darkness; a world now where only desolation, desperation and despondency abounded. But it was to their great credit that they remained calm, remained strong, knowing that they could not reveal their emotions while Rebecca depended on them so much in her fight for survival.

Not surprisingly, though, Sue admitted that it was difficult to control her feelings as emotions ran high. "Inwardly, I was in an absolute mess and just didn't know what to think. I knew she was really ill and there was nothing that Nick or I could do. We just had to put our trust in the medical profession."

Nick's appearance at the hospital in the evenings at least alleviated some of the pressure she had been under, knowing that he could share the burden. The demands at work were such that he had to go into the office, attend meetings and consult with clients, but Sue kept him abreast of the news by telephone from Alder Hey. Most of it so far had been anything but positive, and with the latest devastating developments of Rebecca's life seemingly hanging by a thread, Sue had urgently contacted him.

What he saw when he arrived in the ICU department shocked him.

"I had not been in that sort of place before but when I walked in I was hit by the sound of machines bleeping and blurring - masses of machinery and lots of wires and tubes, and goodness knows what. I got to Rebecca's bedside quickly. We didn't know what the hell was going on and it was frightening. The medical staff had put her on a ventilator to undertake the breathing process. She was wired up to monitors and looked at us totally bewildered, wondering where she was and why so many people were around. It was unreal and we couldn't believe it was happening to us."

The doctors' immediate concerns for Rebecca's condition meant the night time was critical in her fight for life. Sue and Nick kept vigil until 2.00am, the church minister, the Rev David Greenwood, being among the visitors that evening to offer comfort. But then staff suggested they should get some rest in the parents' room that had been allocated to them for such emergencies. It was close to the ICU ward.

Sleep, however, did not come easily, so much of the traumatic day's events going through their minds. It was interspersed with regular checks on their daughter and, when daybreak came, they found their brave little battler had survived. There had been a scare, they were told, when staff took Rebecca off the ventilator after reducing her medication. She appeared to be in good spirits, but then suffered a relapse, stopped breathing, and was quickly put back on the ventilator.

But her fighting spirit had pulled her through against the odds and, after so many setbacks, it was a much needed boost for everyone.

After assurances that nothing untoward would happen to Rebecca in the meantime, Sue and Nick travelled the short journey home that morning for showers and changes of clothing. Nick contacted his office to advise on work-related matters and told colleagues he wouldn't be going in. They completely understood. The pair then hurriedly returned to Alder Hey.

In consultation with the medical team they were informed that further tests had to be carried out on Rebecca. Understandably, their frustrations were growing. It had been three weeks since she was first admitted. She was in a critical condition, was dependent on a ventilator and, without it, could die at any time. This wasn't how they had envisaged life for their daughter, being confined to a hospital bed with tubes and wires everywhere, her life in the balance.

Their uncertainties were further complicated after talks with an ICU specialist and a specialist from the neurology department. They indicated that Rebecca's symptoms may be the result of one of two things. The first was a virus called Guillame Barry Syndrome, where the nerve endings unravel and vital bodily functions are lost, albeit for a finite period. The medics suggested that if that diagnosis was found to be correct a recovery from the illness was possible, although there were no guarantees. Alternatively, the illness was more ominous - a terminal condition - but further investigations were required.

Meanwhile, there were background fears that the longer Rebecca remained on the ventilator the more she would rely on it and stop breathing herself. That would have been catastrophic. Attempts to ween her off it had so far failed, due to her being so poorly, but staff continued to monitor her 24 hours a day for any signs of an improvement.

Life for the Pyes centred around Alder Hey. Sue felt she had to be with Rebecca as much as possible, just being on hand at any hour should her condition improve or deteriorate. Nick called into the office briefly each day, but the parents' room originally allocated to them was to become "home" for almost two months. Occasionally, one or other would slip home for clothing or food, but the priority was being there for their little girl.

"We felt like nomads, really," stated Nick. "After Rebecca became very poorly and was taken to intensive care Sue and I thought it best if I just went in to work for a few hours and do what needed to be done. My firm quite understood and colleagues told me not to worry about work. My daughter was the priority. People within the office and other friends made meals for us to heat up and eat, for which we were very grateful. Shopping was hardly a consideration.

"I felt I should try to be there as much as possible because it was very wearing for Sue to be there all day. With the intensive care department you knew their manning levels were one nurse to one patient and, as such, the attention and care they gave was absolutely superb. But there was still the concern I wasn't there enough really, and I wanted to be there more to support Sue, although family and friends visited during the day to sit with Rebecca while Sue went off to refresh herself.

"Sue displayed a strength of character. Obviously, she was extremely distressed in the early stages, but was able to deal with the great stress she was under. Sue was remarkable in that Rebecca was dependent on a life support machine and without it she seemingly wouldn't have survived, so it took a great deal of courage to put a brave face on things. She was helped by the friendliness and efficiency of all the staff within the intensive care department and developed a rapport with them."

Trying to cope with the stresses of work while his daughter fought for life was almost impossible for Nick.

"It was difficult to give any degree of concentration to work-related matters," he said. "But after the first couple of weeks, and in the knowledge that Rebecca was in the safest hands she could be in, it was probably a bit easier for me because for a couple of hours I was able to immerse myself in work. I knew that at certain times of the day Sue would try to get hold of me to tell me what the position was and who had been to see her. There were basic things that had to be done for Rebecca's general wellbeing, like washing, bed baths and changing, because she had also lost bladder control, so Sue was busying herself doing that. Although it got marginally easier as the days went on, I was always on edge waiting for those important calls from Alder Hey.

"I would try to finish work as early as I could to get back to the hospital and we could actually stay there for as long as we wanted. We usually stayed with Rebecca until the staff changed over and then after speaking to whoever had been allocated to look after her during the night we would go off and have a meal in our room. Then we would return to her bedside for a while.

"Sleep didn't come easily. When we turned the light off at night we lay there thinking about our little girl, not knowing what was wrong with her. Originally, we were hoping it was something of a viral nature. But when it appeared they were leaning towards a severe neurological disorder the hospital told us that there was more that is not understood about the working of the brain than is actually understood, and they didn't have the answers to everything."

Eventually, after further tests, Sue and Nick were informed that Rebecca was showing signs of Leigh Syndrome* which was a life-threatening condition. A second MRI scan had revealed that lesions (or cells) were pressing against certain parts of the brain which would cause the problems she was experiencing, with the brain unable to send messages to certain parts of her body preventing her from breathing in and out properly, not swallowing and not being able to walk - all symptoms of Leigh Syndrome.

Said Nick: "Neither of us had encountered a situation like this with any other family member before. The illnesses in the family followed the more conventional cause, not a very young child falling ill in such a cloud of mystery, and so suddenly. It was very difficult; unreal. We couldn't credit what was going on. Our thoughts turned to us having effectively adopted a seemingly healthy and happy little girl and her coming into our lives and being an integral part with things revolving around her. The thought she might not be with us for too much longer was just too awful to contemplate.

"We didn't really think about ourselves. Luckily, we were in reasonable health. Sue did suffer quite often from headaches just being in an artificial atmosphere for large parts of the day and that was not easy for her. But there were friends who visited at weekends, like Carolyn, who would sit with Rebecca for a couple of hours and we could do what we needed to do. Some of her friends from school and church, people like Philip and Aaron, and Rebecca's cousins, went in to see her and they reacted with her and we were grateful for that.

"As time went on staff tried to reduce her dependency on the equipment to the extent that during the day time, although still wired up to various machines, Rebecca was breathing more or less for herself. But the problems came at night because when it came to her going to sleep the brain just shut off so she had to be put back on ventilation."

The two months Rebecca had been in hospital had seemed like an eternity. But she had confounded doctors and staff with her courage, defiance and determination to fight the illness. It had taken its toll on her body, and on occasions she had flirted with death, but there were signs, just little ones, that thanks to her amazing spirit all was not lost.

For the most part of her stay at Alder Hey there had been few moments to lift the despair her parents had experienced. But they took encouragement from occasions when she appeared brighter, was more aware of her surroundings, of her smiles which greeted family and friends and of her attempts to engage with the play co-ordinators who brought along colouring books, toys and games. In fact, her gradual improvement, at least during the day, enabled her to go with her mum and an intensive care nurse to the park, the promenade and even the cinema. At least it brought a sense of normality for mum and daughter - activities that had never seemed possible at one stage - and lifted Rebecca's spirits even more. Her expressions of joy when she was taken home on one occasion and went out on her slide which had remained idle for so long in the back garden was so uplifting for her mum and dad.

Sadly, Rebecca's was an unusual case, a baffling one for so long, and because her breathing patterns were so intermittent she was in hospital for the long haul. There was no escape from that.

There was no escaping the fact, either, that her condition was a dangerous one and, as such, life expectancy for however long could not be guaranteed.

A specialist warned that she might never be able to breathe independently, even though the medical team decided her dependency on the ventilator could be reduced at night. But in the background loomed the large shadow of Leigh Syndrome. The hospital became more firmly of the opinion that it was that disease which had struck at Rebecca's body. The prognosis was that she would have periods when she was reasonably well, but then she would suffer what they called an 'episode', whereby she would be taken suddenly and seriously ill. What occurred after such 'episodes' was that the patient would not recover to the same degree of health they may have had previously due to the fact the disease was so degenerative.

The heartbreak for Sue and Nick was the realisation that these could strike at any time and Rebecca could die.

Life was for living each day. With all the uncertainty surrounding their daughter it was a philosophy they adopted straightaway.

* Leigh Syndrome is a progressive disease affecting the brain. It is sometimes called Leigh's disease. It is caused by defects in the brain cell's pathway for producing energy. This process occurs in parts of the cell called mitochondria. The defect can involve several different steps in the pathway (e.g. pyruvate dehydrogenase or the mitochondrial respiratory chain). The pattern of inheritance depends on which step is affected: most cases are autonomic recessive but a few are X-linked or show 'maternal inheritance' (due to mtDNA mutations).

Common problems in young children include poor weight gain and floppiness. Later, there may be problems with movement (such as stiffness or tremor), loss of vision, abnormal eye movements, difficulty swallowing or abnormal breathing patterns.

Most patients have problems by the age of two, deteriorate rapidly and die within a year or two. Other patients have a step-wise downhill course starting later in childhood. These patients may deteriorate suddenly and then show partial recovery, followed by periods in which their condition is stable. In the vast majority of patients, there is no effective treatment.

Chapter Four

Life In Turmoil

THROUGHOUT the uncertainty of it all, for both Rebecca and her parents, there was the non-stop rollercoaster of emotions.

Life, they had suddenly experienced, was a fragile affair. The long term consequences of Rebecca's illness was not something to be contemplated at present. For the youngster, it was a case of fighting for her very existence. For the parents, it was being there for their daughter, helping and encouraging her, calling on their inner strengths to remain strong as a couple in this time of stress and trying to maintain an optimistic outlook despite all the evidence to the contrary.

For the time being at least, their life centred around the ICU department at Alder Hey, keeping vigil, worrying, wondering, waiting - and hoping.

Rebecca's sickness and the subsequent investigations that had been undertaken over several weeks pointed towards the diagnosis doctors were now convinced was the right one. But until it was officially confirmed the authoritative speculation was just that.

In March, a muscle biopsy and fluid taken from her spine were sent to Newcastle for tests to determine whether it was Leigh Syndrome. However, the results were unlikely to be ready until early June. It just added to the frustration.

Meanwhile, the day to day routine that Sue and Nick had become accustomed to continued.

"We just had to take each day as it came and not just each day sometimes, but each hour," stated Sue. "One minute Rebecca would be okay and the next she would be really poorly for no apparent reason. We were living a nightmare that was never going to end. There was the uncertainty of what you were going to wake up to each day. We fairly quickly settled into every day life with Rebecca and her disability, but there was so much to do to keep things normal.

"You couldn't get upset in front of her. There were times when I could have sobbed. She would just be lying there like a wet lettuce with tubes hanging out of her, but she was always able to produce a smile for me so we couldn't let her down. It didn't matter about the name of whatever she had. It was the consequences. And all I could think of was: Why Rebecca? Why should she have it? She just didn't deserve it.

"I knew there were no answers to those questions. I don't know who I was angry with, but I was so angry for her.

"After a period of stability Rebecca was one day sitting in a little chair having some lunch when a doctor came to see her. But 10 minutes after he left she started shaking violently and nobody knew what was wrong. They sedated her in the end because she was shaking that badly. They thought it must have been another attack of whatever was happening to her.

"There was another time when she was being fed milk food via a nasal gastric tube which went up the nose and down into the stomach. However, it became dislodged and she aspirated into her lung. No-one knew it had happened and Rebecca seemed comfortable for a few days until one of the doctors said he didn't think her breathing was as good as it could be and they would need to carry out an x-ray. She ended up going to theatre twice in a day - once to get her lung drained and when they couldn't drain it they took her back down a few hours later and removed a small portion of her lung because all the milk feed had collected there.

"It was a case of what else could go wrong, and we found lots of things could. Sometimes we asked ourselves what else she might pick out of the medical book to try? It was our way of making light of things. Not that it was a laughing matter, but I think we would have gone crazy if we had not taken the light-hearted attitude that we tried to adopt. We didn't want Rebecca to see that we were worried. If we could make a bit of a joke of things and make her laugh we thought it would help her. But we just didn't know what might happen from one hour to the next."

From the moment she had been switched to ICU Rebecca had shared a common bond with the other young patients. All had different degrees of illness. Many, like her, were among the more critical, but their courage and spirit was an inspiration to all. The emotional effects for the families were understandable and for Sue, particularly at visiting, coping with it all was not easy. "Occasionally, I would leave her bedside for a minute or two, and when I returned I could see Rebecca had visitors. I just needed a few moments to myself because I couldn't have coped if people saw I was upset. It was something that I didn't like doing in public.

"Don't get me wrong, I was very grateful and Rebecca enjoyed having visits. It was difficult, though, at times in that visitors wanted to know how Rebecca was and generally the ins and outs of everything. But to talk in front of a child who had got perfect hearing and perfect understanding of everything was very difficult. Without being rude to them I was having to try and tell them snippets, but sometimes I was asking myself who they had come to visit - me or Rebecca.

"They tended to talk to me, which was fine, because visitors helped to break up the day. But Rebecca was the one who was needing company. It was alright me being there but you get fed up with the same person, and a four-year-old doesn't want mum all the time. Some of her school friends visited and our neighbour's son, Aaron, came in on occasions and she thoroughly enjoyed his visits. They would get up to mischief on the ward and that was great. She had fun. But other friends seemed to be overawed by it all. Yes, I was grateful for the visits, although some days I couldn't have wished them far enough away."

Initially, the idea of staying close to Rebecca by living-in at the hospital was a good one, but it was an environment from which Sue and Nick needed a break - for sanity's sake. Their 'home' for around a month had been a room in what had originally been nurses' accommodation. It contained a bed, a TV, and there was the use of a kitchen. They had looked upon it as being a stop-gap while Rebecca got better, but the change in her circumstances had brought about a rethink.

"The room was so depressing," Sue continued. "We only lived seven or eight minutes away from the hospital and felt that we could go home, have a meal each evening, do the washing, and a few normal things, and then return to Alder Hey first thing in the morning. So we left the hospital about half eight or nine in the evenings. Friends may have prepared food for us, or we would go to theirs for a meal, and then we would return home, collapse for a few hours, and I would be back in the hospital by eight o'clock the next morning.

"I did not sleep much at times, but health-wise I was fine. I was more relaxed in the hospital than I was at home because then I wasn't with her. The ward round was done any time between eight and nine and I wanted to be there to find out what had gone on during the night, although with her being on intensive care there was a one-to-one situation so a nurse was always with Rebecca. But I wanted to find out what the doctors were saying, basically being nosey, and also so I could tell them about incidents that had occurred as well.

"The nurses encouraged me to leave ICU to have a break which I did, but there was no point going out. I would only wander round looking at the food in the supermarket thinking Rebecca would like that - she was constantly on my mind. I just didn't feel comfortable not being there and I always wondered what I was missing. Even when I went for a cup of tea I would ask a nurse to phone me if a doctor was on the rounds. They must have been sick of the sight of me and made a joke that I should be given my own pass instead of having to ring the bell to get in and out of the ward."

While Sue and Nick awaited the muscle biopsy test results from Newcastle they wanted to learn as much as they could about Leigh Syndrome if, in fact, it was confirmed. At that stage the internet was a relatively new phenomenon, but ideal for researching into the disease, so they asked a friend to check it out. The information provided was pessimistic, especially for a child in Rebecca's condition, but nursing staff told the couple to speak to the doctors as the illness affected patients in different ways and each case had to be dealt with on its merits.

Sue had pinned her hopes on the fact that the findings from Newcastle might be different or, if it was Leigh's, there may be a cure. But there wasn't. It was bad news, which only galvanised her into believing that if there was little more the hospital could do for her daughter she would be much happier at home. She was aware, though, that wherever Rebecca was there was the constant threat of death hanging over her. It was impossible to give the parents any idea on just how long their daughter would live, doctors had said, although they suggested she could survive for another couple of years, possibly longer. But her mum was reluctant to come to terms with the findings.

"Although I knew she had the disease because they had told me, I decided she hadn't and that we would just carry on as normal as we could," said Sue. "We just needed to get her out of the hospital as quickly as possible. I wasn't actually sure at that time how I was going to achieve that but I just wanted to say thank you very much to everyone, pick her up and take her home and get on with it ourselves. But it doesn't work like that."

The nightmare scenario the family had endured over several months had put tremendous pressure on them. Sue, a pragmatist who had suffered the strains and stresses of hospital life with typical resilience, had been there every day for her daughter while Nick had to fulfil work commitments before joining them later. The fact that their relationship was so strong, loving and caring, meant that their daily routine worked and Sue would not have had it any other way.

"I just got on with it," she said. "That was my job. Nick's job was to keep our heads above water so that when Rebecca was home she would have the comforts we all enjoyed. That's how our relationship works. We share everything in that we shared our love for Rebecca equally, but my role was to look after the house and everybody in the house, and Nick, in the old tradition of the husband, was the breadwinner. It wasn't a strain in that sense because that is how I wanted it to be.

"When things were bad I phoned him and he would come. I am very grateful it did work like that because I tend to cope and just get on with things and think about the consequences later."

The couple could not fault the support, co-operation, dedication and friendliness of the staff, but they felt that the longer Rebecca remained in hospital the greater her dependency would be on those looking after her. For

Sue, every minute of every day was vital time spent with her daughter, albeit wishing it was under different circumstances. But while acknowledging the necessity of her medical needs, she feared the long term effects of her little girl being at Alder Hey.

They were indebted to those who were attempting to coax Rebecca, making slow but encouraging improvement by May, to start enjoying simple things like play times, and the response they were getting gave cause for optimism. What is more, it helped to break up the monotony for her mum, in the tedium that was hospital life.

"Sometimes they were very long twelve hour days, yet other days were no problem," commented Sue. "It would depend on how Rebecca was. No two days were the same. There was a very good play specialist on the ward whom I will always be eternally grateful to. She did all sorts of things with Rebecca which people might have raised their eyes at given that she was a very sick child, including hand and foot painting in the bed! In fact, she was happy doing the messiest things she could do. We face-painted with her and we still have a picture when she put paint in a syringe and squirted it at the paper. It was one of the best pictures I have ever seen, fantastic, and she loved it.

"But she was getting too attached to too many people in there and was becoming institutionalised. I didn't realise how institutionalised I had become until I went home. There was always someone to answer a question and I only had to ask where I would get something from and it was there. I was trying to learn as much as I could about Rebecca's care. People were always helping, but my time with Rebecca I regarded as precious. I was there when she said her first word again after coming off the ventilator and I was there when she started walking again. I was privileged to be allowed to be with Rebecca for as much time as I physically could be.

"I joined in with everything and I often was the one covered in paint. We used to read Noddy stories and watch Barney videos - Barney video after video. I always knew if I ever appeared on the TV show Mastermind that Barney or Noddy would be my specialist subject!

"Once the weather improved and Rebecca did not need a ventilator during the day we were allowed to go into the grounds, or go down to the shop. Rebecca would be in a wheelchair and we always had to take a nurse with us. When we got back to the ward we would move the bed from the bay she was in, put some mats on the floor and she could move around. Despite her restrictions and the fact she was still poorly, she proved to be a much travelled young lady, too, completing a couple of 'firsts' for the staff on ICU. It included going to the cinema and theatre and also having a ferry ride.

"During the day she seemed very well and it was only at night that her brain was telling her that when she went to sleep she didn't need to breathe. As a result, they were still having to keep a close eye on her, but eventually they weaned her off the ventilator altogether - and that was when we were able to start thinking about going home."

Such a thought had not been possible weeks earlier as Rebecca remained frail and weak, but there was no doubting the courage she had shown, a testament to her strong will and determination in overcoming so many setbacks. She still faced an uphill struggle but her will to survive when the odds often looked stacked against her brought admiration from the medical team.

Sue made the most of her time in ICU, making mental notes of the nursing her daughter was receiving, watching how staff tackled particular problems, asking medical questions and generally becoming more involved in the day-to-day routines, hoping that the knowledge she gained would be beneficial when it came to looking after Rebecca at home.

"It was a learning curve all round," she admitted. "I never thought of myself as being medically minded or wanting to go into the caring profession, but I learned an awful lot, and fairly quickly. I had to learn how to bed bath because Rebecca was all tubed up on the bed and we used to have to wash her hair in the bed as well. As soon as the poor girl saw the bowl she just cringed because she got absolutely soaked. In fact, we all did, but you had to laugh. We would then get the cones out to say 'wet floor' because the water would go everywhere. Her hair was so long and trying to get the soap out of it when she was lying flat on her back was no fun really. It's a good job the mattresses were rubber.

"I also learned how to feed Rebecca through the nasal gastric tube and how to use the suction machine to clear her secretions from the ventilator. She had been fitted with a tracheostomy in April in a small operation to give her more freedom and allow her to eat and talk more easily. I had to be taught how to change the tracheostomy because staff said I would have to do it eventually, anyway. I remember the surgeon was there, apparently to show us how to do it, along with some nurses who had been trained in the process. But he just turned to me and said I could do it and he would talk me through it and all the qualified nurses just stood and watched! I had no idea what I was doing, I had an audience as well, but fortunately the patient was the model patient. She was superb. She didn't know what was happening and if that had been me I would have been scared stiff. But she let me do it and that was a little notch on my belt.

"Obviously, I had to do it quite a few more times and eventually got signed off to say I was capable of looking after a 'trachy' patient. I was also taught how to use the ventilator and how to resuscitate - just general first aid. Thankfully, washing and dressing her was more straightforward."

The training Sue had received, assisted through her hands-on approach on the ward, made her more accomplished in the various processes of nursing and gave her greater confidence that when her little girl was ready for home she was skilled to fulfil those duties.

Signs were optimistic, too, that the dream of her finally returning home was not too far away. It was only on occasions during the night that she needed the ventilator for short periods to help her breathe.

Sue and Nick's greatest wish was to return to normal family life with Rebecca as best they could and as soon as they could. They had been pushing for staff to come up with an idea of timescale whereby they could leave ICU and return for a short time to a designated ward but, with beds at a premium, the waiting continued.

Finally, news that Rebecca had been allocated a bed coincided with a trip to mid Wales for the family. They had originally booked a week's holiday earlier in the year at a cottage in Corwen with their friends, Jennie and David, and their son Chris. But what had transpired since resulted in them settling for a day out to visit them. The date was Thursday, June 1st - almost four months to the day Rebecca had gone into Alder Hey - and was an important milestone in that it was the first time they had travelled by themselves anywhere without nursing staff since the illness occurred.

"It was a long journey and why we had decided to go that far, I don't know," Sue admitted. "We would probably have been better just taking her home, but in for a penny . . . Inevitably, the weather was extremely wet, but we had a super day.

"We took a lovely picture of Rebecca at a railway station at Llangollen sitting on one of the children's rides you pay a pound for. The smile on her face just said it all. We had done the right thing going out for the day and she was with the people that she loved, and as long as Rebecca was with people that she loved, and loved her, she was happy.

"We walked along the tow path and saw a horse pulling a canal boat and then went on a short train journey. We did so much in that day it was unbelievable - even in the pouring rain - and we really didn't want to go back to the hospital that night. It was going to be the first night I would spend with Rebecca in the hospital in a cubicle by myself. That in itself was not the reason I didn't want to go back, but I thought that as we had managed the day out why did we need to go back. But, of course, we had to."

Having established where Rebecca was sleeping, Nick went home because there was no space for him to stay. That was Sue's first experience of what Rebecca was like overnight.

"She had had an eventful day, was very tired and managed to go off to sleep fairly quickly," said her mum. "That was when I started to use the machines she needed overnight, how to ignore some of the noises, but not all of them. There wasn't a ventilator - they had decided she could cope without it - but there was oxygen if she required it and a machine to measure her oxygen levels. That seemed to go off every two seconds but was purely because Rebecca kept moving her foot, which was where the machine was attached. She just had to turn over and the machine would go off, so it was just a case of getting used to it.

"After a few days of being on that ward I was climbing the walls. I needed to get her home. I had slept on and off but every time the alarm went I was wondering was she all right. My bed was much lower than Rebecca's which didn't help, so I was constantly leaning over to see how she was. Generally, she was absolutely fine, fast asleep, although the machine kept telling me something was wrong.

"We tried to impress upon the staff that we wanted to go home. We had proved to them that we weren't total idiots and we were going to be able to look after her. After a fortnight we were finally given the news we had waited so long to hear. But then it was a mad panic to make sure her bedroom was fitted with sufficient power points to take the equipment that Rebecca needed. Our electrician friend Dave sorted that out for us."

On Friday, June 16, mum and daughter were up bright and early knowing that they had spent their last night in hospital. After a frustrating wait for the medication and checks to ensure they had all the equipment - Rebecca's tracheostomy necessitated a suction machine, both portable and one that ran off the mains at home, plus an oxygen machine - they said their farewells to Alder Hey staff.

"My mum and dad came round and were delighted to see us," said Sue. "We had tea and they looked after Rebecca for me while I went upstairs to sort out her room. I put her to bed because she was exhausted, read her a story and waited until she went off to sleep. I then put her machine on that measured her oxygen levels, only to find that it didn't work! So, in mad panic, and knowing she was at her most vulnerable to stop breathing, I phoned Alder Hey. They told me to go down straightaway for a replacement, so I left Nick watching her as I dashed off to the hospital."

Not surprisingly, Sue and Nick remained on their guard for the rest of the evening. There was no television, hardly any talking, just a concentration on a baby monitor they had been given to listen out for sounds from Rebecca's room. Thankfully, it was all quiet, and all three enjoyed a good night's sleep. The following morning Sue cancelled physio and speech therapy appointments for Rebecca at Alder Hey, simply because she felt it inappropriate to return there so soon after leaving.

Community nurse Jan Rowlands visited them for the first time that morning and struck up an immediate rapport with mum and daughter. "She was marvellous and became our friend," said Sue. "Anything we needed, or she thought we might need, she organised for us. Jan was like our liaison from Alder Hey and told us she or any of her team would visit when required. She came every day for a fortnight just to check on Rebecca and on us as well to make sure we were coping.

"At that stage, Rebecca was walking although she wasn't very steady on her feet. We had been given a wheelchair by the hospital to use when necessary, but we didn't use it an awful lot because we were using the car and she was light enough for me to carry her, anyway."

Sue felt Rebecca would settle into home life again quickly if she adopted as normal a routine as possible. This included going in to school for a few hours some days to see her teachers and friends. The evidence as to the severity of her illness, though, was apparent when Sue dressed her for school.

"She had lost so much weight. She was skin and bone. I put her in a yellow summer dress and I couldn't believe it. It just hung on her and it was like there was a coat hanger in her shoulders. A photograph taken in hospital while she was on the ventilator had been put in our church magazine. I didn't see those machines when I looked at the photograph. It sounds stupid because she had tubes hanging out of her, but all I could see was Rebecca smiling. Her eyes were as bright as anything. But when she got into her school uniform I realised how ill she had been."

Rebecca was thrilled to return to school and a party was thrown in her honour - to welcome her back and also to celebrate her fifth birthday. The mums of some of her school friends had arranged it and JJ, the clown, entertained the children - with Rebecca as his assistant. It was an uplifting experience for her after all her troubles and many photographs were taken.

Her mum and dad organised a super birthday party for Rebecca at home, complete with a Noddy cake. It was attended by family and friends, and they were overwhelmed by the hundreds of cards and presents sent to her by well wishers.

During her time in hospital her weight loss had been of great concern. At one stage it had slipped to 18 kilos, which was classed as malnourished, and it was then her mum decided that Rebecca needed a balanced diet.

"I had been taking meals into the hospital because I wanted her to have all the best foods I could get her," said her mum. "I didn't want her to be having chips and more chips because at that point the hospital didn't have a healthy eating plan. So each night I cooked her a meal at home and I would heat it up in the hospital the next day. It was during this time that she discovered a love for broccoli. She couldn't get enough of it and if you had given her a plate full of broccoli she would have been happy to eat it.

"When she left hospital her weight was around 24 kilos, but as she had grown quite a lot she was still classified as under weight. Later, the hospital put her on steroids and that was when her weight took off, spiralling out of control. Her medication included a mild steroid, methyl prednisolone, plus a variety of vitamins, painkillers, a muscle relaxant because her muscles tended to go into spasm, and blood pressure tablets. So it was quite a cocktail. Apparently, there was no scientific proof that they would help, but the hospital were doing what they could."

During August, Rebecca attended hospital for routine check-ups. It was during one of these that the consultant Sue and Nick had been dealing with in ICU told them that he felt she could manage without her tracheostomy. While it was positive news, her parents were a little apprehensive because it had acted as an air way in the event of anything happening. However, the hospital carried out the process of blocking it off in an overnight stay, and she went home the following day with a plaster over the hole in her throat!

A few days later, the family went on holiday to Wales, staying in a friend's flat in Porthmadoc. It wasn't the relaxing break they had planned as Sue and Nick kept a watchful eye on their daughter all the time, and then it was noticeable her ability to walk started to deteriorate. She was also feeling tired so they returned home early.

Nick went back to work a few days before Rebecca was due to return to Childwall C of E after the summer break. The parents were happy that a carer had been appointed to look after her each day at school.

But Rebecca didn't start the new term in September. One afternoon, the five-year-old fell asleep on the settee. An hour later, when her mum went to wake her up, she couldn't. She was still breathing, but her little body was limp.

Sue urgently contacted Alder Hey and then, despite being in a state of shock herself, drove Rebecca to hospital. The youngster was back in familiar surroundings and remained there until October.

Chapter Five

Our Little Battler

IF there was the glimmer of a light shining at the end of the tunnel Sue and Nick couldn't see it.

Their daughter's illness was difficult to comprehend, difficult to accept and her future so difficult to contemplate. For the past seven months they had been at her side, often exhausted, inevitably frustrated and constantly suffering the heartache of Rebecca's life-threatening condition. It was a shattering experience.

Yet they had remained strong, resourceful and optimistic as they watched their little battler overcome, at least to some extent, every misfortune that had been thrown into her path. And their optimism had been rewarded, too, as Rebecca's frail body had refused to buckle under the severity of the sickness. She certainly was a fighter!

The latest episode which had resulted in her return to Alder Hey was symptomatic of her condition. Despite the seriousness of the situation doctors didn't think it necessary to admit her into intensive care. But another lumber puncture and MRI scan to try and assess why she kept falling asleep was sufficient to suggest Rebecca had suffered a relapse. Sue and Nick prepared themselves for the worst, fearful that the problem may signal the end of her courageous struggle. But it didn't. When she did not respond to any of the treatments it was decided to increase the number of steroids to see whether they could stimulate her. They did, and Rebecca was feeling much better when she left hospital in early October.

After the long and agonising wait for results of the muscle biopsy and spine fluid tests that had been taken in March and sent for examination to Newcastle, Sue and Nick had arranged to travel to the north east later that month to see the paediatric specialist to discover his findings. Before that, Rebecca visited school on a few occasions to see teachers and class friends, and also to meet her carer for the first time. Jane Young had previously had no experience of children with disabilities, but had applied for the role and had been successful. It proved an inspirational decision because she and Rebecca hit it off straight away.

During her first stay in hospital, and once she had shown signs of improvement, Rebecca had begun an intense programme of physiotherapy. It required her to be put in a standing frame, which she hated with a vengeance, and she was also encouraged to use splints to keep her legs straight and give her more strength. But her deterioration was such that by the time the family set off for Newcastle she wasn't walking at all.

As Nick's cousin lived in nearby Whitley Bay they decided to make a long weekend of it so the journey would not be too tiring for Rebecca. Expectations as to the result of it all were not high. Doctors at Alder Hey had intimated what they thought their daughter was suffering from, and their trip effectively was to be given confirmation that the prognosis was correct. But they lived in hope . . .

The doctor they saw specialised in neurological and metabolic disorders. While he talked to the parents he observed Rebecca, who was giving the impression of a toddler learning to walk as she shuffled round his office, using the furniture for balance, but often falling and getting back up again.

It did not take him long to confirm the parents' worst fears, that she was suffering from Leigh Syndrome.

"He told us that he didn't need to look at his notes to tell us she had Leigh Syndrome," said Sue. " Just by observing Rebecca and the way she was acting was enough, but he told us in layman's terms what it was and how it showed in the body.

"Basically, it was all to do with her brain stem and he said it was the only part of the brain that could not be operated on. By saying that, and telling us it was a progressive and degenerative illness, he basically signed her death warrant."

It was the devastating climax to Sue and Nick's anguish after the months of optimism, of hoping and praying, that someone, somewhere in the medical profession, might offer a treatment that could possibly suppress the illness over a long period.

"I had thought that there would be something, even if it wasn't a cure, some way of making things better," Sue admitted. "I knew she would always have a disability but one she could live with and hopefully her life could be prolonged more than the anticipated time of a few years. It was optimism that things weren't as bad, that Alder Hey had painted the worst case scenario, and we would find we weren't in that worst case scenario. That didn't happen."

The original plan was that Rebecca would stay at the hospital overnight for tests but the specialist suggested they would only come to the conclusion he had already outlined. However, the doctor asked Sue and Nick to return the following day for Rebecca to have blood tests.

"The specialist explained it so well and thoroughly that we didn't have many questions to ask him the following day," Sue went on. "As he was talking to us he was making notes. He gave them to us so we could refer to them in the future as we tried to familiarise ourselves with what was happening to Rebecca when she had another illness, and to see if it married up with what he said.

"He didn't give us an absolute answer over how long Rebecca might survive, but he did give us statistics we already knew about - and which didn't make good reading - that if the illness is diagnosed within the first two years of a child's life they very rarely lived past two and between two and four they might live until six. With Rebecca having become ill at four and a half we just immediately took the view that we should try and give her as much as we could in the short space of time we had got with her; and to make her life as much fun and as comfortable as we could. So that's what we did."

They left the hospital, enjoyed the rest of the weekend, and vowed to carry on as normally as they could, knowing there was no special formula as to how they came to terms with the fact their daughter could die at any time.

"You tend to push it to the back of your mind and get on with everyday life," said Sue. "That is what life is all about and you take each day as it comes. We were grateful for the days when Rebecca was able to enjoy them. In the month or so after seeing the specialist in Newcastle, Rebecca was not well. She got chest infection after chest infection and she ended up in hospital quite a bit. It was a case of wondering if the tracheostomy needed to be put back in, but each time she managed to fight off the infection well enough to avoid having it."

Inevitably, Rebecca missed most of the school term, but the build up to Christmas was at least a happy time for her. She enjoyed attending the church's Rainbows group and was chosen to be an angel in her school nativity play. Thanks to her mum's creativity, her new bright yellow wheelchair was adorned with wings covered in tinsel!

"I remember her very proudly wheeling herself into the school hall," Sue recalled. "She was quite chuffed with the way I had decorated her chair, but later she started pulling it all apart because she got bored."

When Rebecca returned to school in January 2001 her wheelchair became a necessity. But the combination of her determination and the encouragement and help from her school friends saw her make brave attempts to walk around the playground, until usually reaching a point when she thought she couldn't go any further, and would fall down giggling in her own inimitable way. It was her way of enjoying the attention - and playing to the crowd!

Despite the occasional chest infection, which made her weaker, she loved school and coped extremely well with her disabilities which had become more evident. There were tell-tale signs of the disease at times, her bouts of shaking making it difficult to hold a pen properly, and also restricting her eating capabilities. So the illness was clearly having an effect and academically the work was beyond her.

The school, though, were accommodating to Rebecca's needs, while her carer, Jane, also played a huge part in her education. She would adapt the lessons to suit Rebecca and keep her attention span, which was short, with a different approach to a specific lesson the other children were also engaged in. Her reading was extremely limited but she fared a little better in mathematics.

"She just coped. And because she coped, we coped," stated Sue. "Here we had a five and a half year old child who was taking all that was being thrown at her and not flinching, so why should we be sorry for ourselves. She wasn't sorry for herself.

"We just felt we wanted Rebecca to have the best of everything and we wanted her to enjoy her life. Someone gave me a piece of paper with the words 'quality of life is precious' written on it and it certainly was. After coming home from Newcastle we wanted to be as positive for Rebecca as possible and we didn't want her to pick up on negative things that might affect her determination, which she seemed to have in bucketsful. Nick and I dipped into those buckets quite a lot for some of the determination she had and it kept us going."

Rebecca's sleep patterns were regularly disrupted through her condition and, inevitably, it affected her parents. Said Sue: "She would sleep for three to four hours and wake up and feel that she had had her night's sleep. The fact that we had only just gone to bed was beside the point. With her only being five you couldn't leave her in the room by herself. She didn't have any concept of danger so it was a case of one or other of us going into her room, putting a video on for her and we would either dose in the chair or lie on her bed for the rest of the night. Her video library became extensive very quickly because she would be quite happy to sit and watch videos and play around with her soft toys. She was quite contented.

"We realised that her brain was waking her up telling her she needed to breathe and needed more oxygen in her body. We didn't realise at the time how it affected her body."

There was the danger that the sleepless nights Sue and Nick endured could have repercussions on their own health, so Jan, the community nurse, was contacted about the problem. She told them they were entitled to some help. It amounted to a night time carer staying at their home once a week from 10.00pm to 7.00am to look after Rebecca - an intrusion, perhaps, but a necessity for all concerned.

"We are quite independent people so were a little bit reluctant at first, but we went ahead," said Sue. "It was very difficult for Nick and I to get used to having someone in your house when you are asleep and they are awake, a total stranger. There was the thought that I would have to put my dressing gown on if I popped to the toilet because I might meet her on the landing.

"Rebecca was delighted with Jackie, our first carer, and she fitted in with us so well. During the first couple of months of her being with us once a week we still didn't get a full night's sleep. I made sure I was up early, dressed and looking my best before going in to Rebecca's room to tell Jackie she could go. But eventually Jackie and other carers used to see me at my worst, when I just dragged myself out of bed to see them out of the house. Occasionally, with one or two carers, we woke up in the middle of the night and a curry or some other strong meal would be wafting up the stairs. At 3.00am they were not things you wanted to smell. But because the carers became part of our lives you just got on with it.

"Nick was somewhat more reserved in that he never saw the carers in the morning unless he got up extremely early, but it was his job each evening before he went to bed to make them a cup of tea.

"On the whole, we were extremely fortunate to have so many good carers and eventually our entitlement was increased to three nights a week. We didn't always get them because of illness or other circumstances, or if Rebecca had gone into hospital and the carer was re-allocated to someone else, so it was a bit hit and miss for some time, but eventually it worked reasonably well."

Childwall C of E School continued to play a pivotal role in Rebecca's development and she loved being there. Her friends were always supportive, involving her in their playtimes despite her restrictions, encouraging her when she wore leg splints to try and walk as far as she could, and she benefited socially. When she wore leg splints her classmates would help her out of the wheelchair and support her as she tried to walk. But in return, her presence taught the other children a lesson in what determination could do and also how to respect those with disabilities. Educationally, however, she could not compete with the rest of her class, learning as much as her brain allowed her to and also how much she wanted to, because her stubborn streak occasionally did not make her the most co-operative of students!

Rebecca had to be accompanied at all times in school and that necessitated her mum being present with her if the carer was off through illness or a family commitment. Being in the presence of others, too, was beneficial for Sue because the school acted as a source of comfort to her. Staff were always concerned as to her wellbeing, appreciating the demands on her time at home looking after a sick daughter were constant.

Considering all that she had suffered, Rebecca was a marvellous example of a happy child, sharing her love and affection, revelling in the opportunities youngsters enjoy, and recognised for her strong character and that wonderful beaming smile. But lurking behind her undeniable courage was the shadow of Leigh Syndrome.

"We pushed it to the back of our minds as much as possible and enjoyed her achievements because she had so many," said her mum. "To some people they wouldn't be achievements at all - they would be every day things - but to her, and to us, they were just fantastic, like walking and taking part in the nativity play at school. She had been in hospital with a chest infection up to the day before the nativity, but she still appeared in the play. So, just little things that most people take for granted that their child will do anyway, but these were achievements for Rebecca. So we tried to focus on that.

"But there was always that little black cloud trying to nudge its way in to say 'just remember, she isn't well', although she didn't get any of the normal illnesses other children got. Most of her class contracted chicken pox, but Rebecca thankfully missed out. However, that black cloud would edge in a little too close sometimes and it wasn't always easy to knock back. You would look at her and see she was absolutely fine one day, but you wouldn't know what she would be like the following morning. When she wasn't well or appeared to have an infection it was just a symptom of the Leigh's illness."

Walking remained an effort for Rebecca. Initially, the 10 minute trip to school had been no problem but now it was more of an ordeal. She was encouraged by her mum to walk a short distance and then make the rest of the journey in her wheelchair. The exertion took its toll and Sue feared she may become too tired for lessons. But the five-year-old displayed tremendous fortitude during a 'walking to school' initiative, determinedly managing the entire trip from home to Childwall C of E once, although it left her virtually exhausted. But it was in her nature to strive, to achieve and succeed.

The concoction of pills - vitamins and steroids - had gradually been reduced but among those taken was one to help her sleep better. Her mum administered the tablets, in crushed form, via a gastrostomy tube attached to her daughter's stomach, which had been fitted during her first lengthy spell in hospital.

But generally, in the period from November to Spring 2001, Rebecca's health stabilised and it appeared the life her parents were wishing for her despite the problems was beginning to be realised. So much so that Sue and Nick's thoughts turned to the possibility of holidays.

It was hard to believe the events of the previous 14 months, how their lives had been turned upside down in the turmoil of their daughter's fight for survival; how they had set aside their emotions - so highly charged as they were - in what had been the most traumatic circumstances to be strong for Rebecca, comforting her, fighting her pain with her and praying for her.

So it was surreal in some ways now to be contemplating holidays. But after so much strife the family needed and deserved to enjoy some much-needed relaxation on their own - away from hospitals, work and the day-to-day torment that was very much part of their lives. So a holiday to Majorca was arranged for April, followed by a half-term break in May with friends to a cottage in Cornwall. What could be better?

Sue, Nick and Rebecca had suffered so much pain that perhaps at last there was a glimmer of light in that dark tunnel. The worst, for now at least, was over - or so they thought.

But their trip to Cornwall became the holiday from hell. Their nightmare returned as they were plunged into new crisis, in which desperate measures had to be taken, and Rebecca was left battling for survival again.

Chapter Six

Emergency Air-Lift

FUN had been in short supply for Rebecca since her illness struck. But the holiday to Majorca changed all that.

There had been disappointment for the family when a planned trip to Ibiza in the August had been aborted on medical advise, but on this occasion doctors at Alder Hey had given their blessing for Sue and Nick to take Rebecca to the popular Balearic islands resort. And what a wonderful time she had!

Although slightly more dependent on her wheelchair, Rebecca made the most of the Palma Nova hotel's play area, using the climbing frame and slides, and making friends with other children during the afternoon kids' club. Her mum and dad had been apprehensive about leaving her there, particularly as they were unsure if the leaders could understand her speech, but their worries were unfounded as she revelled in the various activities.

It was an opportunity, too, for Sue and Nick to relax a little. For so long their lives had been spent on alert, concerned for their daughter, but here she was like any other little girl, happy and content, full of smiles, enjoying the warm weather and making sandcastles on the beach. And the added bonus was that her appetite had been good and she had been sleeping well.

So successful had the holiday been that plans were made immediately on their return for a week's break at a friend's cottage in Cornwall in the May half term with friends Jennie and David.

Rebecca had suffered a slight cold the week prior to the holiday, but she was in good spirits on the drive to the south west. Her medical provisions created extra luggage so two cars were used for the trip and, with the prospect of a seven-hour drive, it was thought necessary to stop off at Exeter on the Friday night.

She was unwell overnight at the travel lodge, but it was decided to carry on to the fishing village of Polruan the following morning. The weather on arrival at Saturday lunchtime was cool so warmer clothing was required for the sail across the estuary by water taxi to Fowey. Rebecca looked out of sorts, caused by what appeared to be a chest infection, so cough mixture was bought for her. She did not sleep very well that night and looked pale during visits to Looe and Polperro on the Sunday. But another disturbed night raised question marks about the rest of the week.

Alarm bells started ringing on Monday when she was sick over breakfast. Sue and Nick took her to the doctor's surgery just round the corner but it was closed due to it being a bank holiday. They rang the emergency number and were told to take Rebecca to the nearest out-of-hours medical centre. Speed was of the essence but pushing the wheelchair from the cottage, situated near the quayside, up the extremely steep hill to where the car was parked proved hard going. Rebecca didn't complain. She just looked forlorn and languid.

Her condition suggested there was a need for urgency, although Sue and Nick hoped that the necessary medication would have the desired effect. But during the journey to the medical centre she started to turn blue and was going in and out of consciousness. All four adults were trying to keep her awake.

"I knew there was something really wrong," Sue admitted. "She wasn't really responding to us. We were chatting to her, she was cold and it was scary. When you are with other people you try to be calm and composed, but if Jennie and David hadn't been there I don't know what I would have done. Inwardly, I was beside myself with worry, but you don't show your emotions and you don't want other people to panic. I was concerned that if Rebecca saw us panicking she would have realised something was wrong."

On arrival, Nick scooped Rebecca up and rushed into the centre with her. Staff took one look at her and immediately telephoned 999. "The receptionist and nurse saw there was a dire problem, and went running off for an oxygen machine," said Nick. "They administered oxygen and she did recover a little, but their concern was obvious."

Within minutes an ambulance arrived and Rebecca and her mum were ushered into the back and were told they were being blue-lighted to the hospital in Truro. Nick, Jennie and David followed, as best they could, by car. It was a nerve-wracking journey. Rebecca was being treated as the ambulance raced along the busy roads, severely congested by bank holiday traffic, while mum comforted her little girl, at the same time trying to be oblivious to the speeds they were travelling.

Sue continued: "The siren was blurring, they were asking me all sorts of questions and Rebecca was getting agitated because obviously she was struggling to breathe, and as she was struggling she was becoming more worked up. Her arms and legs were flailing. It was an absolute nightmare. I am not the best of travellers so I was feeling ill myself roaring along in the back of an ambulance at goodness knows what speeds. I was worried about Rebecca but also worried about being sick in the ambulance when I was not even the patient!

"It was a great relief when we got to the hospital, although I had no idea where Nick, Jennie and David where, how far they were behind us or anything. We were rushed through to the A&E and a whole team of people started working on Rebecca. She hadn't lost consciousness, but wasn't far off it, and they were firing questions at me. I was trying to answer as concisely as possible, but we were still very new ourselves to what was happening with Rebecca and, of course, they hadn't heard of Leigh Syndrome. Then they asked me to leave the room - it didn't make much difference because Rebecca wouldn't have known if I was there or not - but no-one knew her and I just felt helpless. I wasn't able to do anything for her. It was totally out of my hands. I was the one with the information and I was hoping I was giving them the right information. But they kept coming out asking me other questions and I would just say 'ring Alder Hey, they have her notes,' and eventually they did. When Nick finally arrived he tried to answer questions but they put Rebecca on a ventilator because they thought it was the best thing they could do."

Rebecca was taken to the hospital's intensive care unit and a doctor contacted Alder Hey to become more familiar with her background. A decision was taken to evaluate the situation over 24 hours. One logistical problem was that Truro had only two paediatric intensive care beds so there was talk of transferring her to Bristol - the nearest specialist children's hospital.

Sue and Nick were hoping for any sign of improvement, however slight, in their daughter's condition and it came during the night when staff told them they were taking Rebecca off the ventilator and sedating her. It was a bit of good news as they tried to settle in a side ward and get some much-needed sleep. But the respite proved all too brief.

"About 10.00am the next morning, after being off the vent for some hours, she was sitting on my knee and we were reading a story and she started to become very lethargic," stated Sue. "We had just seen the Registrar who had checked her chest and listened to her heart and told us that she would be taken to the high dependency unit. But a few minutes later she was just like a rag doll in my arms. We don't know whether her heart had stopped, but she was taken out of my arms and they started working on her straight away. They threw us out of the room and I don't know how long it was before we went back in, but she was back on the ventilator and fully sedated."

For the parents it was like being back on the rollercoaster, up one minute, down the next. Nick alluded to that when the latest setback occurred. "I remember the nurse came and told us that she was sitting up and asking, as she always did, for food. We were encouraged by that and we went to see her, but suddenly it all changed and nursing staff were dashing round and working hard to steady her oxygen saturations which had gone down to a dangerously low level. It was so traumatic and standing there watching it going on was mind blowing. After she was stabilised I left the room for a few minutes. I had to. I just completely and utterly dissolved because the thought of what might happen was too much to take. They admitted to us after stabilising her that they thought they were not going to be successful."

But within a few hours came a dramatic and unexpected twist in the crisis. Alder Hey's ICU department, having discussed Rebecca's condition with their Truro counterparts, agreed to send a special plane to air-lift her back home. The news was met with tremendous relief by her parents, who later discovered there was one shock drawback in the arrangements - there was only room for one of them on the flight back to Speke Airport (now Liverpool John Lennon International). After a brief chat it was decided that would be Sue, although she was almost traumatised by the thought of flying at several thousand feet in a small aircraft.

"Once again, I felt sheer panic," Sue admitted. "We would be leaving Nick to drive home, which he was more than capable of doing, but Rebecca being flown home in a little plane, being looked after by medics, was a little too much to take in. We had been informed on the Tuesday afternoon that Alder Hey were sending staff down, but it wasn't until the Wednesday morning that we knew how we were getting back. There had been talk that we were going by helicopter which had totally freaked me out, but when I heard it was a plane I plucked up a little more courage."

Despite their stoic characters the past 48 hours had been a dreadful strain on Sue and Nick, whose emotions had again been stretched to the limit. To relieve the tension, albeit briefly, they had been encouraged by nursing staff to go out for a meal on Tuesday evening with Jennie and David, who had returned to Polruan to await developments. The restaurant offered a tranquil setting by a river in the heart of some beautiful countryside and provided respite for the weary parents. Talk inevitably turned to recent events and homeward journeys, with their friends agreeing to return to the cottage, pack everything and lock up.

The following morning Sue geared herself for the flight home. When the Liverpool medical team arrived at midday she was delighted to see familiar faces. They immediately carried out an examination of Rebecca.

After thanking the hospital staff for all their efforts, and after a fond farewell with Nick, Sue, Rebecca and the medics were transported by ambulance to Newquay Airport, just 20 minutes away.

"The hospital were very good and gave me a sedative because I got a little worked up over the fact it was going to be a small plane," said Sue. "I was thinking that Rebecca was going through a damn sight more than I was, although she was sedated and knew nothing of what was going on. She had been strapped on to one of the stretcher boards and we went straight to the plane. The ambulance crew put Rebecca on first and then the medical staff got on. I went to join them but was told I had to sit up at the front with the pilot!

"I didn't expect the plane to be as small as it was. It just fitted us all in cosily. It was the thought that it was a small thing that was going to be up so high. It was very strange. Once we got up in the air the plane tilted a little and you could feel the air under the wings, and being buffeted about a bit. It was like being on a fairground ride as you are going up to the top of the big dipper, except that we weren't going back down again. We were still going up.

"I was looking at all the dials. I was sitting on my hands because I didn't want to touch anything. I didn't say anything to the pilot out of sheer fright. I did look behind and I could just see Rebecca, who was almost directly behind me, and the doctor and the nurse were sitting opposite her, checking on the monitors that were attached. But we couldn't talk because of the noise. They just shouted that she was doing fine, or I got the thumbs up when I turned round, but I suppose after that I relaxed a little and looked out of the window, trying to work out where we were as we got closer to Liverpool.

"It was a glorious day with blue skies, thankfully, and we came down into Liverpool very smoothly. The flight wasn't as bad as I thought. We taxied in and there was an ambulance waiting so we went direct to Alder Hey and straight up to ICU. There was a cup of tea waiting for me, for which I was very grateful."

From Cornwall to Merseyside had taken just two hours. But for Nick, there had been a seven hour drive to face, and on top of that the feeling of helplessness, of not knowing about his daughter's plight and how his wife had survived her ordeal in the sky.

"Sue was obviously the best equipped to go with Rebecca, although she was apprehensive," he said. "They kept stressing that Rebecca would be sedated and safe and her breathing would be done by the ventilator. I remember walking through the corridors following Rebecca, who was on a stretcher, and the nurse holding the oxygen and ventilator, and Sue telling me I had to concentrate on my driving and get home safely.

"It was amazing that they were prepared to come over 300 miles by plane to take her back to Liverpool and we were both overwhelmed by the news, although we were grateful for what they had done at Truro. I stood there watching the ambulance head off to the airport thinking it was an odd thing that my wife and daughter were flying home and it would be some time until I saw them again. I was okay about undertaking the journey, but I was worried that something might happen to Rebecca and I would be in the middle of a motorway somewhere. What could I do? I felt very detached and helpless. But there was nothing else for it.

"I started the journey back to Liverpool within half an hour of the ambulance departing," Nick went on. "I made one or two phone calls to advise family, friends and colleagues at work as to the position we were in. It took an awful long time to get back through Cornwall to the point where we had started the holiday. I drove for about two hours and reached a service station on the M5 near Bristol. I rang up Alder Hey and asked to be put through to the intensive care unit where I spoke to Sue. She told me Rebecca was safe and comfortable and we tried to make a joke of me still being 200 miles away and they being back in familiar surroundings.

"I actually felt better then because travelling the first part of the journey not knowing what had happened was nerve-wracking. The phone call had eased my fears, Rebecca was back in an environment where they were very skilled at treating her particular condition, so the remainder of the trip home was less stressful, although it took another four to five hours. I went straight to the hospital. It was strange to think we had only set off a few days earlier for what we hoped would be an enjoyable holiday, but it had all gone wrong."

It had only been when her daughter was back in the care of Alder Hey ICU, hooked up to the ventilator, that it dawned on Sue what had transpired over the previous few days. And the shrillness of the phone ringing in the ward, with Nick speaking to her from somewhere near Bristol, brought it into perspective.

"That's when it hit me how wonderful everyone had been and how marvellous modern day things were that enabled us to be so close to home in such a short space of time, and the care that had been taken in that time."

Once Nick arrived, the couple watched over their daughter for a few more hours before going home for a welcome night's sleep. The weariness of it all had taken its toll.

Following various tests, Rebecca's sedation was reduced to see whether she could cope without being ventilated, and within 48 hours she was breathing herself during the day, and artificially assisted at night. But this was certainly an improvement.

She soon started to appear brighter, more herself again to the relief of everyone concerned, but with her dependency on the ventilator at certain times doctors felt that the tracheostomy must return on a permanent basis.

"It was quite a big decision for us to agree to," stated Sue, "but we were persuaded by the sight of Rebecca becoming very depressed and not taking an interest in anything going on around her. She wasn't even interested when the play specialist came along, which was very unlike her, but the tube connected to her was going up her nose and down the back of her throat so she couldn't eat and that made her miserable. We knew she was able to eat when she had the trachy the last time, so maybe if she didn't have the huge tube hanging out of her nose from the ventilator - she still had the gastrostomy from which she could be tube-fed so was getting the nourishment - it would mean she could eat normally. After talking to the doctors at length we decided this was the right course of action.

"They put the trachy in about a week after we had returned to Alder Hey. It was a second air way for her. If her brain stopped her normal air ways breathing she still had that safety valve." As a result, the improvement was marked and the spirit and character for which she was noted returned.

Rebecca spent the whole of June in hospital, during which time she had her sixth birthday. A party was thrown by the nurses and she received many gifts, including an autographed football presented to her by former Everton striker Graeme Sharp, who was also visiting other children in the hospital.

It was early in July that Rebecca was considered well enough to go home - but the deterioration in her mobility was obvious. Prior to the ill-fated holiday, she had managed to walk some distances, but now even a few steps were a major effort.

However, her return to Childwall C of E immediately presented another problem. Jane, her carer, was not trained to look after her with the tracheostomy back in place so it meant Sue having to accompany her. She was close at hand, helping out in the office, while Jane remained with Rebecca in class. The situation continued until September when Jane became qualified in tracheostomy care.

"Rebecca enjoyed being back at home and the trachy didn't bother her," commented her mum. "It wasn't something people would relish doing, but she made it easy during the weekly change, unless it became blocked up and then you had to do an emergency change. You think you will never be able to do it but I knew that while it must have been uncomfortable for Rebecca to have it done, she always felt better afterwards. In fact, she was superb about it. Her spirits had lifted, too, and she was happy again.

The family spent a quiet week at Conwy, North Wales, during the summer holidays. Rebecca was now much better, but there were worries over her lack of mobility and her weight was piling on, due to the effects of her condition on her polycystic ovaries.

The new school year saw Rebecca moving into the top infants. Apart from one alarm, when she frightened her classmates, the term was incident-free.

"They were all sitting in class and Rebecca just fell backwards," Sue explained. She had had an 'absence', as they called it, a bit like an epileptic fit without the fitting, which we hadn't experienced before. An ambulance was called because the school didn't know what was happening to her but when we got her to hospital she was laughing and joking."

Thankfully, Rebecca didn't suffer any further major problems at school for some time. Her confidence grew and she began staying for lunch.

One of the admin staff, Debbie, kindly offered to train to look after her while Jane had a break during lunchtime. Little did she know how soon that training would be called upon.

Said Sue: "One day she was having a hot dinner and choked on a chip. I had been washing the car and was soaking wet when I got the call from the deputy head to say Rebecca was having problems with her breathing and would I come. They said an ambulance had been called. Living just round the corner I was there before the ambulance, but Debbie had done exactly what her training had taught her, and when I arrived she was changing the tube and the chip had come out. Rebecca was fine and I knew she didn't have to go to hospital. The ambulance crew checked her over and then she went out to play wondering what all the fuss was about. But poor Debbie was in a dreadful state. She had done what was needed but once the adrenalin stopped pumping she went to bits, but she had done a fine job.

"That occasion frightened a lot of the staff. I don't think they had realised how potentially life-threatening Rebecca's situation was. But all credit to Debbie, she carried on helping Rebecca, although from that moment on she was given packed lunches!"

The future may still have been uncertain, but Rebecca shrugged off the setbacks that occurred. Life for a time was stable and happy and school days became the norm. And she was excited at the prospect of attending two major social events - a wedding and a VIP date in London at which she was to be the guest of honour.

Chapter Seven

Make A Wish

IT wasn't a room as expected. It was a suite. Not your normal type of suite in a hotel. No. This one was festooned with a dozen helium-filled balloons, all in her favourite colours of pink and purple, including one with her name on in the shape of a pink star. There were two teddy bears, courtesy of Harrod's, chocolate treats spread across the table and so many DVDs.

The reservation was for Room 1102 on the tenth floor of the plush hotel in the heart of London. It could have been prepared for the arrival of a film star, TV celebrity or some distinguished foreign visitor. It wasn't. But the Carlton Tower Hotel did have among its guests that day in August 2003 one special VIP - Rebecca Pye.

When she was wheeled into the suite by her parents all three were taken aback. They couldn't believe it. It was just as in a dream. The hotel had been adding the finishing touches to the suite while they had been enjoying afternoon tea in the lounge, rubbing shoulders with the titled and the wealthy, the sheikhs in their finery and other guests.

Sue and Nick were not forgotten, either, as a bottle of champagne and huge bowl of fruit formed part of the greeting in the suite, which also contained a bed for Rebecca with bedding especially for a young girl. On a reality note, the hotel had also provided oxygen for her if she required it during the night.

Rebecca could not contain her excitement. She had been eagerly anticipating this moment for a month, a VIP trip to the capital to see her favourite show at the London Palladium - and it was all thanks to the 'Make A Wish' Foundation.

Her community nurse, Jan, had put Rebecca's name forward to the foundation as a child worthy of being granted a wish and within a week members of the foundation met Sue to discuss the possibilities.

"It was very difficult because Rebecca didn't really ask for anything in particular," Sue admitted, "but she had enjoyed watching 'Chitty, Chitty, Bang, Bang', which was one of her favourite films, and one evening she had been watching Blue Peter on TV and one of their presenters had gone to the stage show to help out. Rebecca was absolutely riveted and, as it was going to be on in London, I just thought she would love to see it, so that could be her wish. Some very nice people had come out to see us and we told them what we thought Rebecca might like to do. They took all our details and three or four weeks later we had a call from a lady from the 'Make A Wish' Foundation to say that Rebecca's wish was going to be granted."

But little did Rebecca, now aged eight, know that her wish was going to include so much more . . .

Originally, the plan had been to travel down by train, but that was aborted because of the train strike that affected travellers that summer. However, they drove to Nick's sister's home in High Wycombe, from where they were taken by taxi direct to the Carlton Tower Hotel.

"We arrived on Tuesday, August 19," said Sue. "It was obvious they were expecting us. The taxi door was opened by a gentleman in a top hat and frock coat, and he knew straight away it was Rebecca. We were all just totally amazed because we were not expecting anything like that. We just thought we were going down to London and would be put up overnight in something like a Travel Lodge. But this was just incredible.

"After seeing our suite and sorting a few things out we were taken for a ride on the London Eye. As it was still fairly new the queues were very long and, being August, you could imagine how busy it was. But we were given the name of a contact who greeted us and then walked us right to the front of the queue and we were given a pod to ourselves."

Rebecca thoroughly enjoyed the experience but it was felt that after the long journey down and the excitement of it all, she needed to rest after tea to prepare her for the fantastic 'wish' day that lay ahead on Wednesday.

The foundation had planned the day almost down to the minute and an itinerary had been supplied, indicating that a car would be waiting for Rebecca and her parents outside the hotel at 9.30am and they would be met by 'Make A Wish' representative Barbara.

Rebecca made the most of breakfast in the hotel's restaurant and was most impressed when a waiter arrived with a jug of her favourite tipple - hot chocolate! Then came the first surprise. After meeting Barbara in the foyer, they discovered that their transport for the day was a white stretch limousine. It was not the easiest of vehicles to get in and out of, especially with a wheelchair, but it was an indication that Rebecca was going to be treated almost as royalty for the day and have a wonderful time.

First stop was the London Aquarium, where Rebecca held starfish and was allowed to put her hand in some of the tanks to feel the fish. She later bought a cuddly dolphin at the shop as a souvenir of her visit. Planet Hollywood was the destination for lunch, which presented a problem. Meals were served on the first floor and the manager was apologetic over the fact the lift was out of order. But this was overcome when three male staff members carried Rebecca, complete with wheelchair, up a large spiral staircase, although her facial expressions suggested she didn't enjoy the ride.

After a pleasant lunch the limo then transported its guests to the Palladium - the highlight of Rebecca's 'wish'.

"We were dropped off at the front door of the theatre," recalled Sue, "and then taken by one of the staff, dressed very smartly in a red waistcoat, to a rear entrance to make it easier to get to the seating area by wheelchair. Rebecca was wearing a pink dress, which had little purple flowers on. We had really good seats for the matinee performance. I had tears in my eyes because Rebecca's face was an absolute picture. She just couldn't believe that there was 'Chitty, Chitty, Bang, Bang', and it was flying. She loved the songs, particularly the chorus of 'The Old Bamboo'. They were singing and dancing and that is what she had seen on television in the Blue Peter programme, so she was jigging up and down in her seat.

"At the end, when the child catcher is caught, tick-a-tape comes down and we collected some of it before leaving the theatre. We were driven back in the limo to the hotel. We went out for a meal to Covent Garden, but spent the rest of the evening just relaxing. We were all totally exhausted. It had been a really busy day. When we got back from the meal we rang room service for a pot of tea - I couldn't believe the price of it.

"On the Thursday a taxi was picking us up to take us back to Nick's sister's, but we had the morning to go shopping and 'Make A Wish' had given Rebecca some spending money to buy souvenirs. So we took a taxi to Hamley's. We told Rebecca she had money to spend and could choose within reason whatever she wanted. The first thing she saw was a large black labrador cuddly toy, and she immediately said 'I want that'. I told her there was another three or four floors to look at, but although we got a few other things she still wanted the labrador. Rebecca said she wanted to call it 'Buster', the same name as our friend Linda's black labrador, whom Rebecca used to take for walks while I pushed her in the wheelchair.

"So the cuddly version became a companion of Rebecca's and wherever we went Buster came with us. Quite often, Rebecca would sit watching television with Buster beside her, along with her other constant companion, Barney. It was wonderful that she had chosen something which was so special. We had been given lots of memorabilia by the Palladium and one of them was a CD of the show songs. I think we nearly wore it out on the way home. We just kept playing it. The whole trip was a fantastic experience for all three of us."

Rebecca's wish had been granted, but it did not end completely in London. While at their hotel a letter had been delivered from a gentleman called Tony, who owns a 'Chitty, Chitty, Bang, Bang' replica which he had made himself. He explained that the foundation had tried to organise it so Rebecca could ride to the show in his special machine. Unfortunately, the arrangements had fallen through, but he invited the family to Blackpool, where he lived, to see the car and have a ride in it.

"He took us on a ride along Blackpool front and then on to Lytham, where there is a windmill (there's a windmill in the 'Chitty, Chitty, Bang, Bang,' story as well)," said Sue. "We took lots of photographs and also a video.

"Rebecca was delighted that she was sitting in this car - it was the most awkward thing to get her in and out of - but she was determined to do it and Tony let her wear his motoring hat with the goggles on, and she also wore a huge smile which we couldn't wipe off her face all day. We also had a picnic. A lot of people were waving at us as we drove along and you could see people following us to get photographs, not of us, but of the car. It was another memorable day."

Thankfully, Rebecca was enjoying a sustained period of reasonable health. After leaving hospital following the Cornwall drama she returned to school. Her carer, Jane, was then fully trained in tracheostomy care and resuscitation and everything that went with it. Occasionally, the youngster encountered problems with muscle control, suffering discomfort and pain with muscle spasms, but the condition eased after six months through medication. It was simply another reaction to Leigh Syndrome. Christmas was not a great time health-wise, either, but her parents decided she could be looked after as easily at home as in hospital.

Rebecca revelled in social events. They were among her happiest times amid the many setbacks that were part and parcel of her life. She loved meeting people and loved occasions when she was surrounded by family and friends, and so her invitation to a wedding in May 2002 was certainly something to look forward to. Nicola, the daughter of Jennie and David, was marrying Simon at Allerton URC. The hope, of course, was that Rebecca would be well enough to attend. But the week before caused more stress for her parents.

Four days before the wedding Rebecca was bouncing on her bed as she was getting ready for school. Her mum told her she might hurt herself, but at the same time recognised that it was something she could actually do which gave her some freedom of movement. But suddenly Rebecca lost her balance, fell off the bed and cracked her head open on the window sill, as her mum looked on horrified. "There was blood everywhere and it was like the Chainsaw Massacre! She bled profusely and I rushed to get loads of towels. I quickly got her dressed and took her to the walk-in centre," said Sue.

It led to an embarrassing situation for her mum, who had only been to the centre a few weeks earlier after Rebecca had wheeled herself off a step at her grannie's house and scraped her face and loosened one of her teeth.

"We had only taken her to the walk-in then as a precaution," Sue continued, "but here we were again with Rebecca in the wheelchair and blood pouring from her head. It had eased a lot but her blonde hair was covered.

"As soon as we got there they recognised us from the month before and I was inwardly really worked up and worried. We got into the cubicle and the nurse looked at her. She asked me to wait, although I didn't quite catch every word, but I thought she said she was going to get a social worker. I thought 'Oh, my God, they are going to take Rebecca off me. It's not my fault she had split her head open, and this was the second time I had been there in six weeks. They are going to think I am neglecting her'. Of course, she hadn't said that at all. It was me getting worked up, mis-hearing and putting two and two together and making five. She had only gone for an assistant to help her because she needed to stitch Rebecca's head. I would have been petrified by the thought, but Rebecca was ever so good."

The head wound required five stitches. Instead of wanting to go home after being cleaned up, Rebecca insisted her mum take her to school so she could show off her stitches to her friends. At least the accident didn't prevent her attending her first wedding. She had a superb time, looking so pretty in a pink dress and carrying a pink, fluffy handbag, which seemed to amuse numerous guests. Her stitches were mainly hidden by her spur-of-the-moment decision to wear her mum's hat for most of the day.

Generally, 2002 was a fairly uneventful year, in stark contrast to the holiday air-lift episode of the previous year. In fact, family holidays to Wales went off without incident.

By this time, Rebecca was among many children from Merseyside and the north west experiencing the wonderful work of nursing and care undertaken at Claire House Children's Hospice based in Wirral. She spent occasional weekends there, giving her the opportunity to mix and play with children suffering severe illnesses like her own, and Sue and Nick were indebted to the staff for their dedication and devotion to making Rebecca's times there so happy. The hospice relies on charitable donations and Sue was eager to raise funds for them. She encouraged her friend David to join her on the annual 15-mile Wirral Coastal Walk, in which thousands take part to raise money for chosen charities, and Rebecca was also keen to be involved. So they pushed her for nine of the 15 miles in her wheelchair before her dad picked her up.

"They met us at the finishing line so Rebecca could rejoin us and pick up her certificate," said Sue. "We all enjoyed it because it was a lovely sunny May day. Rebecca had been given a balloon at the start of the walk and it kept getting caught in the wheelchair. I don't know how it didn't burst, but it didn't, and she still had hold of it at the finish. But we did quite well and raised a fair amount of money for Claire House."

The weather remained warm throughout that summer and Rebecca made the most of her time, whether on holiday with mum and dad or just playing contentedly in the garden with her friends from next door, Aaron, Rachael and the triplets. It had been 15 months of relative calm after the Cornwall storm, for which Sue and Nick were grateful, although they were only too aware that they were still living on the edge, with their daughter so vulnerable to a condition that could erupt at any time. They acknowledged that, but were also greatly encouraged by the fact that Rebecca was still defying the prognosis given by Alder Hey's medical team and the specialist in Newcastle of her survival chances.

Sue maintained a fundraising theme for Claire House that year by organising a coffee morning and bring and buy sale at the church on Saturday, September 27. It proved a huge success. Many of Rebecca's school friends attended with their mums and the hospice provided posters to advertise the event. There was a special atmosphere in the packed hall and people's generosity helped to raise the magnificent sum of £1,000. Another one held 12 months later raised a similar amount.

It was almost as if the disease had retreated into the background, but any thoughts of becoming complacent about it were quashed when Rebecca spent part of Christmas 2002 in Alder Hey with a suspected chest infection, which was later earmarked as a part of Leigh Syndrome. And, as if history was repeating itself, her parents were involved in another dash home five months later as their daughter's health concerns increased.

It was a weekend in May during which Rebecca was staying at Claire House. Staff there had suggested to Sue and Nick that while they were looking after her they may take the opportunity to have a short break themselves. So they took their advice, booking in to a country hotel just outside Shrewsbury with Jennie and David. They had taken Rebecca across to the Wirral on the Thursday afternoon and arranged to meet their friends later that day.

Friday was spent shopping in the town before having dinner at the hotel. A call to Claire House confirmed that Rebecca was having a good time. Over breakfast plans were made to spend the day in Ludlow. The weather was perfect on arrival so it was decided to tackle the local pitch and putt course.

The game had almost finished when Nick received a call on his mobile. It was bad news from Claire House. Rebecca had collapsed at lunch. She was stable on oxygen in her bedroom and staff were monitoring her but were unsure as to whether she should be in hospital. So they requested Sue and Nick return immediately.

"Ludlow was about two and a half hours away," Sue pointed out. "We jumped into the car, dashed back to the hotel, got our car and raced back as quickly as possible, arriving at Claire House at 2.30pm. She was semi-conscious and really didn't have a clue what was going on so we decided to call an ambulance." That in itself produced a complication, as Sue explained: "Because Claire House is on the Wirral the ambulance only had jurisdiction there, so we had to get special dispensation for the ambulance to travel through the Mersey tunnel to take Rebecca to Alder Hey. Normally, the ambulance should take the patient to the nearest hospital but, as we had found out in Cornwall, there was no point taking her to a different hospital when she would only have to be transferred later. We were blue-lighted through the tunnel and traffic was stopped. I was in the ambulance with Rebecca and a member of the Claire House staff while poor Nick was in the car again.

"We were taken to A&E around 5.00pm and were eventually moved to ICU because Rebecca was needing quite a bit of oxygen to keep her levels up. They didn't know what was wrong with her so they put her on the ventilator just to see whether that would help. But she kept pulling it off, which meant she didn't need it. Within 48 hours she was much improved and two days after that we were discharged and went home. It just seemed to have been a blip. No-one knew the reason. It was all part of her condition."

In terms of her illness, the rollercoaster ride had taken another downward spiral, though fortunately not hurtling out of control. But it was followed by an upward thrust a few months later as she received the VIP treatment on her 'Make A Wish' dream trip to London.

In her short life Rebecca had achieved several firsts, mainly through the extent of her medical condition. But 2004 was to bring another first on an occasion which provided her with one of her greatest thrills, make her parents so proud and bring tears of joy to everyone who was present.

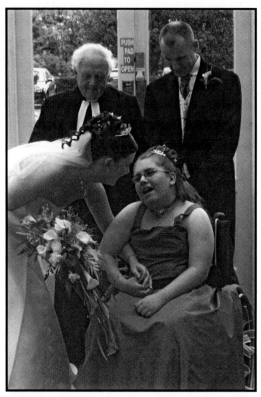

Bridesmaid for Carolyn - 'What a joyous day'

Centre of attention - Rebecca with her dad (left), David and Jennie on holiday in Majorca

Father Christmas was a favourite with Rebecca

Holiday fun - more laughter in Ibiza

'Let's dance' - trying on her new dancing outfit

Proud medal winner

Rebecca, aged three, with her best friend, Barney

Rebecca, her dad and Barney on her fourth birthday in Ibiza

So cute - Rebecca, aged four

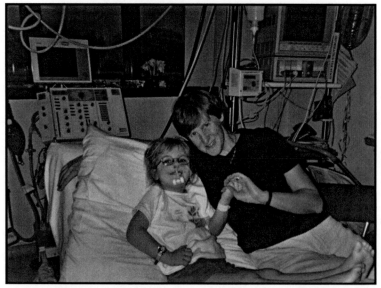

Still smiling through - Rebecca and her mum are surrounded by machinery at Alder Hey Children's Hospital in March 2000

The happiest bridesmaid ever

Time away with Jennie, David and Chris in Wales
after another stay in hospital

Chapter Eight

The Bridesmaid

AFTER the latest scare Sue and Nick vowed not to take any further weekend breaks when Rebecca was at Claire House. They simply couldn't chance it. The drive back from Ludlow to Shrewsbury and then to the Wirral had been nerve-wracking, not just because of the journey, but the thoughts that constantly nagged at them concerning their daughter.

When Nick received the call from the hospice it had been another stunning reminder of the fine line she trod. It had come out of the blue and they found themselves so far away, isolated, unable to offer comfort, and desperate to be back by her side.

"We didn't know what to expect as we drove back," admitted Sue. "Part of us thought that, knowing Rebecca, she would be sitting up wondering what was going on because nine times out of ten it was just a blip and she would pull through as she always did. But there were the odd occasions when Nick and I would look at each other and say 'do you think that she won't'? There was no reason why she wouldn't this time. But we were still pretty shocked when we got back to the hospice seeing her so poorly."

It was hard to forget, too, the prophetic words from the medical profession who had been so pessimistic of her survival chances beyond the age of seven after she had bravely overcome the initial problems that had placed question marks over her ability to pull through at all. It was the black cloud analogy that occasionally lifted a little but always hovered overhead, and it was something the parents had grown accustomed to live with.

But despite the fears that surrounded each passing setback there remained the optimism - there had to be for sanity's sake - as Sue alluded. "We went through a phase when we kept thinking 'she's past seven, it could happen any time'. Then we thought that she had got this far, so perhaps the medical people had got it wrong. There was no firm evidence that she couldn't survive longer and I quite often used to think to myself that they had got it wrong. At times we asked for another MRI scan of her brain to see if things had altered on her brain stem; to determine if the scarring had changed. I knew it would never go away but I wanted to know whether it had stayed the same with all the little episodes she had suffered - and were they episodes that had progressed the illness or had it remained stable. I believed that if it was going to stay the same for that length of time she was going to be able to carry on indefinitely. But we were told there was no point in doing another scan. The medical profession knew they had the right diagnosis, but I suppose you just hope and clutch at straws.

"If I had been brave enough when we saw the consultant on our four-monthly visits I would have asked 'what if?', but Rebecca was always with us at the consultations and I didn't want to discuss that sort of thing in front of her. I could have phoned him instead, but a telephone conversation isn't the same as seeing someone face to face and reading their body language to assess if they were positive about something or not."

However, such was the way that Rebecca embraced life, refusing to allow the bad times to suffocate her spirit and determination, that those around her couldn't be depressed for long. Her very presence, her smile, her giggle, her love, wouldn't allow it.

There were tears. Oh yes. But at times they were tears of joy, especially at moments when she was at the heart of social occasions.

Rebecca described Carolyn as "one of my bestest friends in the whole wide world." In the youngster's eyes she could do no wrong. When Rebecca was seriously ill for the first time, Carolyn visited her in intensive care on Saturday mornings to play or read with her while mum and dad had a break. She always had a little present for her, too. Considering the age gap - Carolyn was 25 when Rebecca was four - their friendship flourished.

"As soon as Carolyn walked into intensive care Rebecca didn't want to know anyone else, so they built up a very close bond," said Sue. "Carolyn also babysat for us and trained to look after Rebecca with her trachy and, basically, Rebecca just loved the bones of her. But Carolyn then got herself a boyfriend and naturally we didn't see as much of her as Rebecca would have liked, but she kept coming round to sit for us.

"We were delighted when Carolyn got engaged to Trevor, although Rebecca didn't understand what engaged meant and I had to explain it to her. She asked me if we would be going to the wedding like we did when her younger sister, Nicola, was married and I said I am sure we would be invited. But what I hadn't told her was that Carolyn had asked me if Rebecca would like to be a bridesmaid. My immediate reaction was 'yes', but I asked her not to say anything to Rebecca because I didn't want her getting excited."

Rebecca was nine at the time and the wedding was still 11 months away, in June 2005. Her mum felt it would be better waiting until the new year to tell her when the possibility was more realistic. Naturally, when Carolyn eventually broke the news to her she was thrilled. It was to be Rebecca's first time as a bridesmaid.

One of the first priorities was to find suitable dresses - she was the youngest of four bridesmaids - and that entailed trips to Chester for Jennie (Carolyn's mother), Carolyn, Rebecca and her mum. It also presented a problem, as Sue explained. "We found something that was suitable, but we could only get the skirt part for her because of Rebecca's shape. The bridal shop was very good and got in touch with the company that supplied the bridesmaids' dresses and they despatched a length of material. Jennie was then able to make a top that fitted, so Rebecca didn't look any different from the others, which was lovely.

"Next stop was a date at the hairdressers. Carolyn wanted a trial run to see if she liked everyone's hair the way she wanted them to have it on the day. I was more nervous than Rebecca because normally she didn't like people messing with her hair, but she sat so still. She had it all put up so it was decided that was how it was going to be. However, by the time we got home it had all fallen out because Rebecca's hair was heavy. So it was modified slightly.

"As the big day neared she got extremely excited. We bought some little silver ballet pumps for her and also some silver ribbon to put on her wheelchair to make it look more presentable.

"When the weekend arrived she did not really know what she was going to be doing. All she knew was that it was going to be special and Carolyn and everyone she loved was going to be there - and she knew she would be on show and Rebecca didn't mind that. We had spoken to her about it and how she would have to be on her best behaviour because so many guests would be looking at her, taking photographs, and she would have to smile. We decided to stay for two nights at the Hoole Hall Hotel, near Chester, where the wedding was being held, because we felt we didn't want Rebecca to be rushed. We enjoyed a meal on the Friday evening and just relaxed."

Mum was more nervous than Rebecca on the Saturday morning, with some justification, as her daughter was the first bridesmaid to have her hair done at 9.00am - five hours before the ceremony. But she need not have worried. She was so proud of her hair she didn't touch it once. Photographs were taken of her even before she put on her bridesmaid's dress and so many people told her how gorgeous she looked. Sue washed and dressed her, adding some make-up to make her look more grown up, before placing her in the wheelchair and arranging her dress. Rebecca then went to Carolyn's room, where the other bridesmaids were assembled, and the bride presented them all with little silver heart necklaces to wear. Rebecca was very proud of that and also the little tiara in her hair.

If her mum was already near to tears over how beautiful her daughter looked, her entrance to the banqueting hall for the wedding must have opened the floodgates. It certainly caught Sue by surprise.

"We were all sitting waiting for the wedding to begin," she said. "I don't know who was the more nervous between Jennie and me. Jennie's daughter was getting married but I was worried that Rebecca might have one of her choking fits or something.

"When the music began Chris, the bride's brother and an usher, walked down the aisle first pushing Rebecca. I just filled up then because I wasn't expecting that - the bride usually comes down first - but I realised it was done so they could get Rebecca into position. I thought she may get bored but she behaved well and enjoyed the ceremony. We had taken her walking frame with us so she could stand up on a couple of the photographs.

"Carolyn and Trevor had a blessing in the conservatory part of the hotel and everyone was smiling, but Rebecca did a good job of cute smiling. Then she danced the night away and it was after midnight when she went to bed. But she had had a super day. On the Sunday we went to Chester for a walk and then returned to the hotel for lunch with everyone who had stayed over."

But there was a sting in the tail for Sue and Nick . . . as Rebecca completed the day in Alder Hey!

"Whether it had all been too much for Rebecca, I don't know, but she had a roaring temperature," stated Sue. "We got home about 5.30pm and it was a case of early to bed after her big weekend. I popped round to my mum's, leaving Nick in charge, but he rang me and said Rebecca was burning up and would not settle. I returned home, dosed her with medicines, but as she was shaking we thought we would take her to hospital. Thankfully, they said it was only a high temperature, so it was probably all down to the excitement of the wedding.

"She was only there a few hours but I thought it ironical that there always seemed to be a trip to Alder Hey involved in whatever we did. However, she was fine the next day and returned to school. But we had so many lovely photos and memories of that wonderful weekend."

It must have been most satisfying for her parents that Rebecca was growing up into a lovely young lady. But it was noticeable, too, that she had become more aware about herself, her body and the constant supervision that was necessary, either during the day or at night. Her development, in some respects, was more advanced than her contemporaries and against all the odds was approaching her final year at junior school. There was no doubt when younger that she was happy to have carers watch over her at night, but her attitude changed.

"As she got older she felt it was an intrusion," her mum said. "She didn't want other people dressing her in the morning, combing her hair and putting it in bunches, or telling her what to do. She wanted me to do it. Normally, Rebecca would be dressed for school when the carer left around 7.30am. I suppose she was realising that it wasn't something everyone had done for them so why should she be different to any other young girl who didn't want everyone to see her body and to change her and wash her. To a certain extent I think she became embarrassed that she had things done for her.

"I put myself in her position asking that if it were me and I was that age would I want a total stranger to be doing this to me and the answer was a definite 'no'. So I tried to make it as easy as possible and spoke to the carers and they quite understood."

One facet of Rebecca's illness was her weight gain which began with the number of steroids she was prescribed when she became ill at the age of four. Later, it became exacerbated by her love of food and the restriction in her movements, resulting in her having to crawl upstairs on her hands and knees.

"I always encouraged that because it was a bit of exercise for her," Sue continued. "We did have a stair lift which she used to like putting her soft toys on and giving them a lift up and down. But as she became older, and a lot less mobile, we had a through floor lift put into the house in which she could go up and down to her bedroom when she wanted. But we didn't use it an awful lot because, as a cruel mother, I would make her crawl up the stairs. It was only when she was very tired or had a bout of illness that she would go in the lift, and even then only reluctantly.

"When she tried to climb the stairs you would always have to be behind her because sometimes she would just misjudge putting her hand down or her knee in the wrong place and she would come sliding back down again, usually falling on me, and it would be me in a heap at the bottom of the stairs, not her."

Other provisions had to be made in their home, too, including a hoist in her bedroom on the grounds of health and safety for the carers when they helped her in and out of bed, while Rebecca was given a hospital bed, complete with a control to move it up and down, which she had great fun operating!

A hoist was also erected in the bathroom to make it easier at bath times, but often Rebecca would do her best with mum's help to accomplish the task without using the mechanism, albeit in a slightly less dignified procedure.

It was a lifestyle in which her parents had to adapt just like their daughter. At one time it was relatively easy for Sue and Nick to go out for the evening leaving her in the capable hands of a babysitter. But after the illness, and with her restrictions over manoeuvrability and weight gain, plus the knowledge required to use the tracheostomy, there were fewer people they could call upon to look after Rebecca.

"I think Nick felt it a little more than I did because Nick liked to go out," Sue admitted. "I am a home bird. It was enjoyable to go out and very good of family and friends to sit with Rebecca but if we weren't able to get a sitter it didn't bother me. I had what I wanted. I had my family unit. So it was just a case of adjusting and enjoying what we could when we could.

"When she started to go to Claire House I hated it. Rebecca enjoyed it, but I felt they were doing my job. When Rebecca was at the hospice we did things because we had the opportunity of doing them but I never really felt comfortable. I preferred doing bits at home with Rebecca, but she got an awful lot from Claire House. She didn't always want to go there but she saw children in a worse position than she was.

"Rebecca was very caring towards them as some were desperately ill, while I don't think we ever looked upon her in the same light. When you saw her you thought that she was just a child in a wheelchair. More often than not she looked well, was bright and cheerful. She communicated and interacted with people, whereas a lot of children at Claire House unfortunately couldn't. So it was good for Rebecca to be in that situation."

Jane, her carer, was a qualified sign language teacher and helped Rebecca to learn the basics of a language called Macaton, based on signs and words. However, she only used it occasionally because she wanted to talk normally, and was eager to make herself understood, particularly to the people who mattered.

And she had a mind of her own, too, when it came to fashion as her mum often found when shopping for clothes. Rebecca's size made it difficult at times to find suitable clothes - but the youngster definitely knew what she wanted.

"If I picked something up and said that it was nice she would say 'no it is not' and picked up something she liked," said Sue. "She was comfortable in jeans and T shirt but it was difficult to find clothing that was suitable for Rebecca at her age because of her weight problems. She was in ladies size clothing long before her friends were so finding something that wasn't too old and too frilly was a headache. But in jeans and T shirt she was the same as other kids.

"At eight, she was already wearing aged 13 to 14 clothes. It was a combination of medication, lack of activity and the fact she had polycystic ovaries, which is a major cause of weight gain. But we didn't know that until she was 11.We had restricted her diet hugely thinking it was the fact she was just not mobile enough and we were trying everything to keep her as mobile as possible.

"Rebecca had this appetite which was part of her problem because she didn't know when she was full. Her brain wasn't sending a message to the stomach saying 'you've had enough'. She would just continue eating. She had lost so much weight when she first became ill and was actually classed as malnourished as you could see every bone sticking through her skin. Then when she started eating again we were delighted, but we couldn't win because the weight started to pile on. And there was a phase when she had a bad case of reflux so every time she ate something she would bring it back. But the weight gain continued even though she wasn't getting the nourishment. The reflux lasted for four months, stopping as quickly as it started, but again it was down to the Leigh's problem."

Not surprisingly, after her long association with Alder Hey, Rebecca didn't take too kindly to hospitals. There were certain clinics she had to attend, but her mum was never sure whether her daughter was going to co-operate on these visits. As a result, Sue always had a supply of headache tablets which were a necessity to ease the stress during appointments. But on days when physio was concerned her demeanour was far more positive, enjoying the games she played which were actually stretching her limbs, making the physio girls laugh and being the centre of attention. Clinics to her, though, were a different proposition and the shutters would come down.

Rebecca was happiest at home or on holiday with mum and dad. Her parents knew every minute of every day was precious and just seeing her develop despite all that had happened brought the greatest satisfaction. Reaching the age of 10 was another milestone and family and friends joined in the celebrations. It was a case of forgetting what the future might hold and live for the day.

Decisions, though, lay ahead. She was preparing for her final year at junior school and Sue and Nick confronted the problem of where their daughter would best be suited to continue her education. Another question concerned Jane, her carer, and whether after the excellent relationship she and Rebecca had built up at Childwall it would be allowed to continue when she moved schools. But these were happy worries in the sense that Rebecca had overcome so many health issues.

Her life was that much richer for having such wonderful parents, but her one concern was that she didn't see as much of her dad as she would have liked - and sometimes she told him! Nick was conscious of that as he fought a constant battle with the dilemma of his demanding job, commitments elsewhere and trying to spend as much time with his daughter as possible. But he regarded their relationship as an extra special one . . .

Chapter Nine

Being Together

REBECCA was never going to succumb to her illness without a fight. That was obvious.

The evidence as to her strength of character had come at the tender age of one year and dad was on the receiving end. Nick had been feeding her at lunch and they had a difference of opinion over whether she should eat cauliflower cheese. Rebecca thought not and the vegetable was aimed in his direction!

At the time, he still could not believe his good fortune at being the father of such a lovely little girl, a baby who had quickly adapted to her new life, but who had undoubted spirit.

For Sue and Nick the experience of adoption had been a special event, the question of whether they would be matched with a boy or girl never arising. It hadn't mattered. What mattered was the enjoyment Rebecca brought into their lives and how elated they had been when they had first set eyes on her.

After the illness first struck, and during the subsequent periods when she was poorly and returned to hospital, the emphasis was on being together as much as possible. Being a solicitor did not offer opportunities for regular hours at work, resulting in Nick constantly juggling priorities, and invariably working late.

"I always tried to get to the hospital in time to have half an hour with Rebecca each evening, and then at weekends we spent as much time with her as we could," he said. "After the serious early stages of her illness and in order for her to come home we had to undertake first aid and medical courses and learn about resuscitation. I remember thinking at first that I would never be able to do it, dealing with the tracheostomy, changing the tube and learning about suctioning. It didn't come easily but it was important for us being together again. She was glad to be at home because she felt safe and knew she was as well as she could be.

"She had healthier periods from the age of seven when we adapted to what we could do through her being wheelchair bound. We did things she liked - having picnics on trips to Wales or just going shopping in town, when it was a condition of Rebecca's that we called in at Marks and Spencer's so she could have a hot chocolate which she adored.

"In the times she wasn't well you didn't want to think of the consequences. It was too awful. But the question: 'How many more years will we have of this?' was always in the back of your mind. The specialist we saw in Newcastle and then on an annual basis used to say how remarkably well Rebecca was doing. At one meeting he told us 'Go for it. Who's to say she could not live until she was 40'. I thought that would be absolutely wonderful. So we lived for the moment and enjoyed what we could. We always had a day together at the weekend as a family and nothing much would interfere with that."

Of course, there were exceptions, like the times when her dad went to see Liverpool playing. She developed a strong dislike of football - it took dad away from her for a time - and she and Nick exchanged banter when it came to a match clashing with cartoons she wanted to watch on TV. And if he spent a few hours at work during the weekend she would give him the thumbs down and say 'boring'. But it never affected the special relationship they built up.

"When we were in London with the 'Make a Wish' Foundation, I remember there was a song in the musical in which a little girl was singing 'I've got you two', and Rebecca was sitting there and knew the words and she got hold of our hands and sang 'I've got you two'. It was the security of the family unit.

"There were many people she was happy to be with other than us, like gran and granddad, and once she was dropped off there it was her outing and we were not very popular when we turned up to collect her. We had certain friends trained to deal with her particular needs, like David and Jennie and Lyn and Dave, and she was quite happy for us to go out when either of those couples were looking after her. She had quite a lot of fun, too, playing and coaxing more drinks and biscuits out of them."

Time together was so precious that the family made the most of holidays, usually going abroad. "Rebecca always seemed to travel well and we did get more adventurous, going to places like Majorca, Minorca, Corfu and Tenerife," said Nick. "It was quality time and she was pleased to have David and Jennie with her. I wouldn't say necessarily she was daddy's little girl. It was the fact that the three of us were together - that is what Rebecca regarded as being the most important - and she was in the environment she wanted."

The week at the Uyal Hotel in Puerto Pollensa, Majorca, in 2004, was particularly significant. It was the family's first time away since Rebecca had the second of her tracheostomy operations. Alder Hey had suggested a location within a two hour flight due to her oxygen levels possibly being compromised, and also the need to be close to a hospital, just in case.

It was something of a gamble for Sue and Nick but, accompanied by David and Jennie and son Chris, it proved an inspirational week. It was one Sue appreciated, too.

"We played on the beach, bought Rebecca her first rubber ring and took her in the water," mum recalled. "She was in her element and thrived in the heat. She was happy and content to crawl down to the water's edge and sit there and let the water lap over her legs. It was relaxing for us, too. She was happy and she was well. I was happy we were away. We had lovely evenings when we walked into the town centre and Rebecca enjoyed a milk shake.

"She was always an early riser so Rebecca and I would get up about six in the morning and walk along the promenade. It was a lovely time just to be together before the bustle of the day and we used to talk about what had happened the day before."

The success of that break was the incentive to return to the island the following year for a fortnight, this time staying in the resort of Cala Bona. But it was not without its problems.

"We were flying from Liverpool Airport and going through passport control with Rebecca in a wheelchair took a few more minutes," said Sue. "They had to check the chair and also her suction machine, which they had never come across before. But what we hadn't noticed was that her speaking valve from the 'trachy' had come off. I had a spare one with me but it was in the luggage which had already gone through. Despite searching round and taking Rebecca out of her chair in case it had slipped down we couldn't find it. The little cap helped her speak and prevented her 'trachy' from getting dirt in it. So we flew to Majorca without it. However, friends from Rebecca's school were coming out the following week and my dad took a spare valve round to them to pass on to us.

"When we got off the plane I noticed there was something wrong with the wheelchair because it was not running properly. We had bought it because it was lightweight and she could manoeuvre it herself. We had paid a huge amount of money for it and it had obviously been damaged in the hold. But the hotel were extremely good because they found someone on the island who could repair it to a certain extent. So for the first week we pushed Rebecca round in a hired wheelchair, without foot rests and a lap strap to save her from falling out, so we used the strap from a suitcase instead.

"Rebecca spent much of the holiday lying on a lilo in the children's pool or in the sea on a new tyre we had bought her, surrounded by four adults in case of an accident. Again, she thrived in the warmth so it was another superb holiday."

Rebecca, now 10, had one more year in junior school before moving on. Where she would go was the dilemma. Sue and Nick didn't want her to be under pressure. They preferred somewhere that offered a happy environment where she wouldn't be judged on academic achievement. The size of school and the need to learn life skills were also key factors. Local girls' secondary schools, where he friends were going, were considered and then rejected simply through her inability to cope with the work. However, the special needs school at Sandfield Park, West Derby, offered the perfect solution and they were more than happy to take her. And, in March 2006,

Rebecca received official confirmation that she would be continuing her school life there.

The city council, though, got their wires crossed and when all parents received letters indicating which school their child would be moving on to Rebecca's name was down for Gateacre Comprehensive. Sue immediately contacted the council informing them that as her daughter had special needs she had been accepted at Sandfield Park. They thanked her and said they would amend their files.

Rebecca's long blond hair, gorgeous face and captivating smile, made her particularly photogenic, and she became used to cameras clicking in her direction. It was no wonder therefore that Claire House Children's Hospice chose a photograph of her in a fundraising campaign. It was taken when she was aboard a fire engine during one of their fun days and she also featured on a video with her mum and dad to emphasise the importance of the Wirral hospice for the whole family.

Another photograph of her adorned a wall in the hospice for several weeks. It was taken when a group of children went strawberry picking one day. Clare Doig, a staff member, explained: "Mike (Stewart) had lifted her out of the wheelchair to do some picking and she was adamant that she hadn't eaten any. She was laying back among the strawberries covered in strawberry juice around her face. We took a picture of her and we will never forget that. Afterwards, as soon as you mentioned Rebecca, people would say 'oh, strawberry picking', because we had her picture up for ages. That was a moment when you say 'thank God I work here', because you just feel so humble."

Rebecca was always a popular visitor to the hospice, situated in Wirral countryside close to Clatterbridge Hospital. Her first visit was in September 2001, arriving with mum, dad and cuddly favourite Barney, and she usually spent six weekends a year there. Unlike other youngsters suffering life-threatening illnesses, she had fewer restrictions in the activities that were organised.

Said Clare: "When you looked at Rebecca, she was just like a normal child. She was in a wheelchair and had a tracheostomy but that never stopped her from doing anything. Compared to other children she was a lot more able. When she first came she was walking and she could talk, which a lot of our children can't . That's why I think so many staff wanted to look after her because you did get so much back from her.

"Rebecca wasn't really a girly girl and always preferred her hair in a pony tail. But when she was here for a 'Princess' weekend we had people coming in to do things for the children and she looked absolutely beautiful. She had her hair pinned up in curls, was wearing sparkly make-up and had a feather boa round her neck. She just looked like a princess. Every time we had a weekend like that and dressed the children up the staff would end up in tears. She enjoyed watching everyone else, was very much a people person, but was also nosy and wanted to know what was going on."

Being in a new environment without mum and dad can be quite intimidating for a child but she adapted quickly during initial visits and soon got to know the staff. And always had her favourites, too.

"She fell in love with Mike, one of our health care assistants," Clare went on. "He was brilliant with her, just mad, which she loved and he was a big lad so he could pick her up and do rough and tumble with her and every time she came she asked if Mike was about. She loved other people as well but those two had a special bond, and he adored her. She just shone and made people want to talk to her because she was so lovely, fun-loving, a little cheeky at times, but her personality was wonderful."

Staff found it tricky to restrict Rebecca's appetite because she was so fond of her food. "She loved her meals, and chocolate cake and puddings, in particular," Clare continued. "They come here for fun and when everyone else is sitting eating a pudding it was so hard to say 'no' to Rebecca. She enjoyed baking, too, but that was because she wanted to eat the ingredients before they had even gone in the oven! You had to watch her like a hawk because her mum would tell us after visits here how many pounds Rebecca had put on."

The facilities at Claire House are excellent and Rebecca always looked forward to visiting the light room, a place equipped with interactive buttons or just somewhere to chill out. Her sleep patterns were often disrupted, but as long as she had the company of Barney and the Barney video she was content.

Staff arranged some exciting outings for the children, including a visit to the circus in Blackpool, but a memorable one for Rebecca was the Chester

Zoo Dreamnight, which she attended with her parents and other families linked to Claire House on a beautiful summer's evening.

"You knew it was special because we were invited for six o'clock and the zoo closed normally at five," said Sue. "We were greeted by numerous staff and Rebecca was given a bag which contained all the information, some little treats and a disposable camera. She also received an enormous helium-filled balloon in the shape of a tiger's head. She was delighted with this as tigers were her favourite animals and her favourite colour was orange."

After being put in small groups the children were each asked about the animals they most wanted to see and a little more time was spent at those enclosures. Thanks to the gentleman showing Rebecca's group around, she was taken to a vantage point to get a good view of the tigers.

"It was wonderful to see the children enjoying themselves and seeing everything without having to queue and without the general public," added Sue. "The police, fire brigade and army personnel were present and the youngsters could sit inside the fire engines and ring the sirens. The zoo also provided a packed supper for everyone, too. As we walked around it was so peaceful and you could see tiger heads bobbing up and down in the air with the balloons attached to all the wheelchairs.

"As we left Rebecca was handed another goody bag which was full of animal books and a cuddly tiger. We took home one tired but happy young lady and a bundle of happy memories. It was certainly a Dreamnight."

The hospice, opened ten years ago, was originally a 10-bedded unit offering accommodation for six children with life-threatening or life-limiting conditions for up to18-years-olds and parents and families to stay with their child. Four years ago a teenage annexe adding four more beds and parent facilities was built, allowing the age range to increase to 23 years.

It totally relies on charitable donations, trusts and corporate involvement towards the upkeep and it costs £2.6million a year to fund the operation. Local celebrities from the worlds of sport and entertainment increase its profile and offer help but the biggest support comes from the general public.

"It is 24 hour nursing care," said Karen Roberts, head of care. "We have a range of specialists - physiotherapists, music therapist, activity co-ordinators, aromatherapist - and a hydro therapy pool so children have the opportunity to swim. We provide a range of facilities and activities for siblings and look after the whole family, generally. It is about working in partnership with the parents because sometimes it is very hard to leave your child. But it is also about giving them a break and the chance to spend time with siblings who can get forgotten because of the time spent caring for a sick child.

"Sue and Nick have been huge supporters of Claire House and with Rebecca have assisted on the fundraising side, putting our name forward as beneficiaries at so many different events. We offer a home from home environment, and families say it's their hotel. It's a free service, they are looked after and it takes away the daily stress of being in your own home. We provide their meals so parents can spend quality time with their children."

Rebecca made a huge impression on everyone there and was known as a very affectionate child, always wanting or giving hugs. She loved being at Claire House, but on every visit would tell staff how much she was missing her mum and dad!

Chapter Ten

A Caring Relationship

JANE YOUNG knows what it's like to be at the centre of a crisis. When you are trained in the role of a carer you have to expect the unexpected. But it still does not prepare you for the emotional consequences it can produce.

Despite all the professionalism that is associated with the job the effects can still be heart-rending, occasionally reducing you to tears, and leaving you a physical wreck.

They are the days you wish will never happen, but you know that when they do you have to call on your experience and handle the situation with calmness and control.

Jane did just that when Rebecca suffered a choking fit during one of Mrs Owens' lessons at Childwall C of E School. It had only taken a split second for her to turn round to reach for the suction machine but when she turned back Rebecca was under the table on the floor apparently unconscious.

"I realised she was out for the count," Jane recalled. "I looked at the teacher and said 999. She asked the other pupils to stand up. They were only six years old and behaved brilliantly, marching out when Mrs Owens told them to. I had the suction going but I knew there may be some other kind of problem because all the secretions were flying out and I was using catheter after catheter. Then this lady appeared out of the blue and held Rebecca (she was an off-duty intensive care nurse, a parent of one of the children at the school who just happened to be there). I carried on suctioning but she was going bluer and bluer.

"Then Rebecca wet herself and I thought 'that's it, this child is dying in front of my eyes and there is nothing I can do - I don't know what to do'. Then suddenly she just started to come round and the paramedics arrived. By the time she got into the ambulance she was laughing and joking . . . all in the space of 20 minutes. We went to the hospital, met her mum and then her dad arrived.

"Later when I returned to school from the hospital the staff asked how Rebecca was and I said she was fine. They also asked about me and I said I was okay, then burst into tears. I looked a right idiot. But I shook all day and all night. I went to night school that night and I could feel myself trembling all the time. It had been an horrendous experience, absolutely awful, but at least Rebecca was alright. A week later she choked again and the suction wasn't working so I used a foot pump. I was thinking 'don't do this to me'. It wasn't as bad as the first time, but it was still pretty scary."

Fate played its part in bringing Jane, originally a nursery nurse who had worked in the private sector for many years, and Rebecca together. She had left her job to bring up her own children but once they were of school age she was eager to become involved in care work again. She became a dinner lady for a time before a friend told her about SENIS - Specialist Educational Needs in School Support. Jane applied for a job with them, was successful, and was told that she would be looking after a child at Childwall C of E School - a coincidence given that her children were educated there, she was familiar with the set-up and knew some of the staff.

Jane was informed that the little girl in question had specific needs and required speech therapy, occupational therapy and physiotherapy. She also discovered when attending the school for the first time in September 2000 that Rebecca was unwell and in hospital, so she was assigned to another youngster at a different school.

However, their first meeting proved an eye-opener for Jane, who saw a frail child, vulnerable, but one with spirit.

"Sue said she wanted to go and speak to the head so I said I would sit with Rebecca," said Jane. "It was story time so I read to her. She was this tiny little blond thing with glasses and a very soft voice. You could hardly hear it and you had to concentrate to understand what she was saying. She had splints on and was wearing boots so we took the boots off before reading the story. When I tried to put the boots on she was kicking out because she didn't want them on, and I thought this was a girl with a bit of a will. But she was very good, so sweet and lovely."

It can often take some time for a relationship to develop, particularly when the child has serious health problems, but Jane felt from the outset that their friendship would blossom, and it did. For the most part, she was by Rebecca's side during the school day encouraging, helping, sometimes cajoling, and adapting the teacher's lessons to suit her capabilities. She got to know very quickly Rebecca's likes and dislikes, what motivated her and what she could achieve. And then there was her sense of humour, occasionally mischievous, and her enjoyment for life.

"She could do her work, she could count and there were certain words she could remember from prior to being ill," Jane continued. "In the afternoons there might be a story or the children could watch television. She liked television at home but found films in school boring so she would ask if she could sit on my knee. She was five then and often she would fall asleep.

"Although her ability in class wasn't marvellous she was still on a par with some of the others, the less able children, when it came to numeracy and literacy. They would have set groups and the work would be differentiated through the classroom. She could do what the rest of her table could do number-wise and writing. She was good at stories and she would answer questions verbally. If you wrote something she could copy and was quite good at her level, but unfortunately her level didn't improve very much. She would do her work as best she could and loved painting. Her hands usually got covered in the stuff, too!

"Because I couldn't leave her I took a cup of coffee into the classroom and she would ask if she could have a taste. I told her at first she wouldn't like it, but surprisingly she did, and I always left a little bit at the bottom of the cup for her to finish. It was an unusual drink for a five-year-old."

Jane had been aware of Rebecca's illness before their first meeting and admitted that the information that outlined the issues had made horrifying reading. But Sue had made it clear to her that Rebecca, in the main, should not be treated differently to any other child, either from a work or behaviour point of view. Generally, she was a gentle child, but there were occasions when her character changed and it was only later discovered that these changes were brought about by a form of fits.

Working so closely on a day-to-day basis with Rebecca meant that Jane inevitably became more attached to her - a situation, a colleague pointed out, that may have devastating effects, given the youngster's life-threatening condition.

"I never used to think about how long she would live and I was speaking to someone at a Christmas party who used to do a similar job," Jane recalled. "When I told her about Rebecca and what a lovely girl she was she told me I was too close. But I thought it was too late for that. You couldn't not become close to her. As for the prognosis, at first I wondered what I might do and how I would handle it. I was more worried it might happen when she was in my care, but we just took every day as it came.

"I had this rapport with Rebecca. She was like one of my own. It was like that. She had a cracking sense of humour, a wicked one at times, so you could always have a laugh and a joke with her. Sometimes you would get cross with her but sometimes she would have you in hysterics. We had relaxing times, too, in the brilliant little sensory place we created in the resource room. We went with her mum, armed with school money, and bought lights and a type of fish tank which we put on the wall (it wasn't real) and the fish moved up and down. There were big cushions and a foi fur throw, and we would snuggle down there. We were always singing and messing about. She did grow up and knew how to behave and what liberties she could take, but she was stubborn and if she didn't want to do a thing she wouldn't."

Jane became used to the fact that Rebecca might be in intensive care in hospital in the morning for some reason, but be back at school in the afternoon. She adapted her approach to Rebecca on how well she was feeling and to what extent she could achieve physically and mentally.

Although Rebecca was wheelchair-bound generally when they first met, Jane would hold her by her coat and help her to walk around the playground with other pupils. At one end of the school yard were tree stumps which she would sit on to play with her friends. Her spirit to overcome her disabilities were such that she often surprised both her carer and classmates, and Jane remembered the day she marvelled at Rebecca's endeavour.

"It was after another bout of illness when she couldn't walk. She had gone home for her lunch and when she came back I was standing in one of the classrooms with my back to her and Sue asked Rebecca to show Mrs Young (that was my school name) what she had been practising. As I turned round Rebecca stood up and walked towards me. It was lovely to see her walking again. She didn't have any help and managed a few steps."

Jane went on: "After I got the tracheostomy training I could actually change her tube on my own. I must admit I became very good at it, not panicking or anything. When her mum first started going home I felt a little bit like 'don't leave me on my own', but there was only ever that little bit of anxiousness. I was never drastically worried, but I don't know why, because I should have been.

"When they increased the size of Rebecca's tube I accompanied Sue to the hospital. The other tracheostomy allowed her to speak, but when they increased the size there was nothing, no sound. So she would lip read or do a little bit of 'sign', which I taught her. She had a good memory for that. It went on for a week or two and when the nurse came in to school to put a clean tube in, she said she was going to change the size again. It was lunchtime and I said that I would return in half an hour. When I came back the nurse had changed the tube and as I walked in Rebecca said: 'And about time, too. What time do you call this, Mrs Young?' I just burst into tears. I hadn't realised how much I had missed her voice. Although it was a very quiet voice at least there was something there, and after a week of silence it was lovely to hear her again.

"I can't say she was one of mine, but she was like a member of my own family. That's how it felt to me. I was with her six hours, maybe more, each day. She got the cuddles and the chastising, just like mine."

Undoubtedly, Rebecca thrived under Jane's watchful eye at school, but she benefited, too, from a combination of Childwall being a happy school, the staff being so caring and her classmates so encouraging. Unwittingly at times, Rebecca's presence commanded attention at school - girl friends loved her long, silk-like hair and the variety of bobbles and ribbons that adorned her golden locks - and her bubbly personality, her smiles, her laughter and friendly nature were also so appealing. Philip, Aaron and Alex, in particular, remained firm friends throughout her junior school life and the party Philip organised for Rebecca's birthday and farewell from Childwall underlined the esteem in which she was held.

The whole environment of life there helped Rebecca to thrive and play an active role in school activities. And head Diane Shaw believed that her personality was the key ingredient in making friends and attracting people to her.

"Everyone just loved her," she said. "You couldn't fail not to and that says it all. It was Rebecca who did that, instigating and insisting she was at the centre of things. The children were a lovely group and took her to their hearts and they did everything they possibly could for her and with her. They would take it in turns to be with her at lunchtime and playtime; take it in turns to talk and play with her, to keep her smiling, and also tell her what was going on at times because her sight was limited. So they learned very early on how to care for somebody - and that was the secret.

"Rebecca was one of those very special people. When she came back to school on a more full time basis that smile just melted people's hearts. So she, herself, did the majority of that relationship building. The children had already known her before her illness and then when she was restricted in her movements and what she could achieve they rallied round and were a fantastic year group that went through school with her.

"The school is a very special place and I don't say that lightly," the head went on. "There is an air of care and love which I am really proud of and it is something that was started by Frank Driesson (previous head). That love and care was surrounding Rebecca the whole time she was here. We knew about the long spells she had to have in hospital and we knew we needed to adapt the school to suit her, and that she was a priority when it came to looking at access for her. We gave her as much support as we could and the school was always there for her and mum and dad. We always wanted to know how things were going, and my door was always open to them, and particularly to Rebecca."

Mrs Shaw, who has been Childwall's head since January 2001, had been informed of Rebecca's health problems by Mr Driesson during discussions prior to taking over, although at that point a diagnosis had not been made. But the school, built in 1988, quickly had to adapt to Rebecca's needs once it was obvious that she would be relying more and more on the use of a wheelchair, providing new toilet access and widening the doors into classrooms plus, of course, the creation of the relaxing sensory room.

But one door that could not be customised was the one in the head's room. That, however, did not prevent visits from Rebecca, whether social or for other reasons.

"I struck up a very good, strong friendship with her," said Mrs Shaw. "After spells in hospital she would always come to say hello. Jane brought her down, usually with one or two of her friends, and I would give her a big hug. I know teachers aren't suppose to have that sort of contact with children these days but I think in this case if she hadn't had her hugs Rebecca and I wouldn't have had the relationship we had. She was one of my kids, a determined character - and very stubborn. But when she looked at you with her lovely big eyes, I would think 'how do I tell her off'. Afterwards, I would go away really upset, but Jane would say to me that Rebecca needed to hear it.

"She was such a strong influence. She had an aura about her and you knew she was in the room. She was either with you, or she had switched off, and in many cases she would be doing her own thing, especially if it was maths, because she hated maths. Sometimes you knew she didn't want to be there. But she made sure she was involved, even if not at the centre of everything, and especially at Christmas, which she loved, and her birthday."

Mrs Shaw acknowledged Jane's presence as vital in Rebecca's schooling in what was effectively a dual role as carer and supplementary teacher. "We were very lucky because she had Jane, who helped her through the educational side of it as well. We adapted lessons, and there were other things she could do, like PE. She could still catch a ball and hold a hockey stick. Jane was crucial to that. We would not have been able to manage without her."

Those close to Rebecca could understand her when they engaged her in conversation, but other people naturally found it more difficult. However, she had a special gift of communicating through her eyes and her smile, and the head had no doubt that she was a child of exceptional qualities, not just through her personality but her persistence in striving to achieve despite her restrictions.

"She was a very special child in that no matter what pain she was going through and no matter what issues she was going through there was always a smile on her face - and that is unique. She knew she was ill but it didn't seem to bother her.

"We tried to get as much support as we could through other schools. Harold Magnay School were fantastic. A taxi picked her up on certain days and she would go with selected pupils, who were her friends, to the ball park there and have fun. We even at one point tried to take her horse riding, but that didn't work because the more she sat on the horse's back the more it aggravated her arthritis. It was a great shame because she loved animals and cuddly things."

Mrs Shaw recalled the "ooh, ah, isn't that wonderful" occasion when Rebecca, playing the role of Mary in the school nativity, was wheeled in carrying the baby Jesus, and the visit she made with classmates to the Everton FC Study Support Centre, where they enjoyed working on computers and undertaking a music workshop. It culminated in a special dance at school based around the work Rebecca was doing and it was attended by some of the football club's directors and one of the officers from the local authority, all of whom were impressed by what they saw.

Such was the school's ethos that support extended beyond the children and staff, and Mrs Shaw recognised the importance of keeping in close touch with Sue and Nick.

"It was a rare diagnosis and the prognosis wasn't good. Rebecca's mum had come in to explain to me what was likely to happen. Faced with that sort of information, and being told to me by someone who was being so brave, I was just blown away by the courage and tenacity both Sue and Nick displayed over that because she was such a precious child.

"I realised that there was a possibility Rebecca's life could end while she was still here in school. It is one of your worst nightmares as a head to have to deal with that and the aftermath of it. I needed to make sure there was a support structure in place so as a Christian school we were prepared. So we had bereavement counselling for all the staff, including the mid-day supervisors, because she was very much part of their lives as well. She had been very poorly when she was in Year 2 and spent time in hospital. We used to keep the children informed all the time when Rebecca was in hospital, and she was always in our thoughts and prayers. But because many of the children were so friendly with her themselves, they would come and tell me how she was.

"As each year went by we kept thinking we were so lucky to have her. And then when she actually moved on to secondary school I just thought 'wow, this child has reached 11'. I like to think that we as a school gave her that incentive to want to keep going."

The end of summer term 2006 was a poignant time for all at Childwall C of E. There had been the special party for Rebecca and other leavers as the school prepared to say farewell to them as they moved on to further education. But there was that tinge of sadness, too, particularly in respect of Rebecca, who had played such an integral part there, a larger than life character whose bravery and resilience in the face of such a debilitating illness had been so inspirational.

Mrs Shaw believed Rebecca's move to Sandfield Park School opened up so many more opportunities for her.

"I almost at one point suggested Rebecca had another year with us. I would have been quite happy to have kept her, but I don't think it would have been good for her. She needed to move on, because they could offer her so much that we couldn't. They gave her the chance to do so much more with the sport. But it was quite a wrench, especially on Monday mornings when I did collective worship. You would look round to see where Rebecca was and it took me a few months to realise that she was no longer here with us."

Chapter Eleven

Sporting Heroine

MOVING to a new school can be both exciting and traumatic. There's the six-week period of summer holiday to contemplate what lies ahead and then, as the first day dawns, it's the facing up to a completely different environment from the one children have been used to - the change of scenery, new teachers, new friends, new curriculum, new expectation.

It was a new era for Rebecca, too, but so different from the situations thousands of other youngsters found themselves in. For there she was, at eleven, preparing to attend Sandfield Park School for the first time when, in reality, she shouldn't have been there.

In their wildest dreams her parents could not possibly have believed their daughter would have survived to become a secondary school pupil. She wasn't expected to live much beyond seven, according to medical opinion, after defying death in the days when she first had to battle the illness at the tender age of four. But whether through courage, determination, spirit, character, or a combination of them, Rebecca had steadfastly proved the experts wrong. So far, she had lived life to the full, remained so happy in the face of severe limitations, and family and friends were so proud of her.

But while there was the usual nervousness for Rebecca in anticipation of her moving schools there had also been additional worries for Sue and Nick. They were used to complications. After all, they had been part and parcel of life for the past seven years, but now they faced the possibility of their daughter being isolated at school without her carer by her side. Continuity for her was vital, but the concern emerged during the latter days at Childwall C of E. Jane Young had automatically assumed that as Rebecca was moving on she would be going with her. So did Sue and Nick. But Jane's bosses had told her that the school she would be attending had their own staff. However, the matter was resolved satisfactorily after discussions between the parents, Sandfield Park and SENIS.

The other anxiety, though, was that Rebecca had recently started new medication and she was suffering from the effects, so the early days at her new school were difficult, to say the least.

Her sleep patterns, always irregular, had become particularly disturbed and fears mounted over her weight, too, which had started to escalate. The hospital had decided to put her on a new drug in August 2006, weeks before the switch to Sandfield, which they thought would suppress her appetite, but unfortunately it also suppressed her system. She became lacklustre, totally disinterested in everything going on around her and was immediately weened off them.

The start of the new term even provided a twist. Her friend Aaron, attending a school in Gateacre, informed Sue and Nick that Rebecca's name had been read out on his class register on that first morning! Nevertheless, she was safely installed at Sandfield, with her parents satisfied that while she may take time to settle in to her new surroundings she was at the ideal school.

"It wasn't an easy start for her going to a place where the only person she knew was Jane who, fortunately, was still going to be her carer there," said Sue. "We had managed to persuade the local authority to let us keep Jane, purely on medical grounds. This was very unusual. I think it was the first time it had ever happened that the carer had gone from primary to secondary school with a child. But it was vital for Rebecca because I think it would have been too much of a change for her.

"I don't think she would actually have coped without Jane because it took Rebecca a long time to settle at Sandfield. She hadn't been very well over a period because she had been put on a new form of medication. Things had not been right, it had suppressed her completely, and she always looked spaced out and wasn't very receptive to anything different. We had also had a new night time carer as well, so everything was new to her.

"The situation over Jane had worried us because Rebecca didn't take to change very well. We would have fought tooth and nail if we had had to if the decision had been that Jane couldn't go with her. But we were fortunate Jane did go because that was one less thing for Rebecca to cope with. Going to secondary school for any child is a huge leap for them, but in this instance it meant Rebecca wasn't special any more. She was on the same footing as every other child in the school - they all had problems - and she had to make her own little mark.

"The school wanted her to be independent. Obviously, there were great limitations on her independence, but they wanted her to be able to do things to the best of her ability. This meant that Jane had to take a step back and Rebecca had to fend for herself a lot more, which she found difficult because everyone had done for her at primary school."

At Childwall, Rebecca only had to drop a pencil and willing hands would rush to pick it up. But in her new school it was a case of learning to communicate and asking for assistance if she wanted something. It was all about developing her independence levels. Similarly, lunch times saw her queuing with other pupils and making decisions on what she was going to eat - and asking for it. Quite often, she took the easy way out and ordered what she had eaten on previous days, but Jane often suggested she made alternative choices.

Famous fighter pilot Douglas Bader, who lost both legs in a flying accident but still became a World War Two hero, opened Sandfield in 1961. He was well known for championing the rights of people with disability.

Approximately 70 children, some of whom have life-threatening, life-shortening conditions, attend the school which was originally designated for physical disability. Now it encompasses a wide range of physical disabilities, learning difficulties and complex medical conditions and has a high ratio of staff, a school nurse and physios on site. It also provides education for Alder Hey Children's Hospital and home tuition for children who cannot attend school for medical reasons.

Jane recognised from the outset that the onus was on determining pupils' capabilities and playing to their strengths. With spacious classrooms and corridors Rebecca was expected to push herself around, but her carer always had to be in close attendance in case Rebecca required tracheostomy care.

"I couldn't leave Rebecca. Even getting to and from school she needed an escort who was trained so I went with her in the taxi," she explained. "We tried to encourage her to speak to the other children, but she always gravitated to adults. She was clingy and often feigned sickness, but it only happened in the half hour I was having my lunch. So they would bring her into the medical room, where the nurse would fuss all over her, and then they would call me. When I asked her what was wrong she would sigh, and when I told her there was nothing wrong she just laughed.

"The school eventually tried Rebecca out with a power chair which was hysterical. She never looked where she was going, she crashed in to everything, then the chair wouldn't move because the footplates would bend in and jam the wheels. But she eventually got the hang of it."

Naturally, Rebecca became frustrated at times and revealed rare moments of temper. On one occasion when she refused to do her work Jane told her off for being rude and she argued back. The head heard her so Jane told Rebecca she would have to sit outside the classroom until she calmed down and apologised.

"When I looked out after a short while she had gone," said Jane, "taking herself to the far end of the school into the maths teacher's class with tales of woe. She was full of sobs and sighs, but there was nothing wrong with her. She was sent to the head who told her off and then she promptly apologised when she came to see me. Yes, the hormones had kicked in by then, and she turned into a banshee, but it was short-lived. She could throw proper wobblers, but then say 'I am so sorry, Mrs Lung', because she couldn't say Young!"

Although her health remained reasonably stable it was only after Christmas that she really settled down, and while it was hard work for her, she became more accustomed to what was expected. But as Easter approached Rebecca started attending an after-school sports club with her mum, as Jane's role ended when school finished for the day. It was a niche that gave her more confidence and she started to excel in the various activities.

Said Sue: "She just loved it. I went along, much to Rebecca's annoyance because she didn't want me there, but it worked out because I would also help with the sports."

Rebecca was selected with others to take part in an event in Manchester with a view to representing the north west team in sport for the disabled. The approach was professional as each child was medically assessed to attain their ability and then categorised, and she proved quite accomplished in the ramp ball and target bean bag disciplines and won a couple of medals. It earned her a place in the team for the competition in Blackpool a couple of months later, but any chance of preparation for that receded dramatically when Rebecca was rushed back in to hospital.

"Sunday mornings in our house were always very relaxed for the first few hours, and then it was action stations as we got ready to go to church," Sue continued. "This Sunday was no different. Nick was getting ready upstairs and was going out a little earlier than Rebecca and me. Rebecca was sitting in front of the television eating an apple, and I was just getting ready to brush her hair. I went into the hall to get the brush and as I walked back in she took a sharp breath and started to choke. I grabbed her suction machine and took off her speaking valve and gave her a few back slaps, but she was going blue. I called Nick and told him to dial 999. In the meantime, I did an emergency tube change just in case the tube was blocked or the piece of apple had by-passed the tube. Taking the tube out can cause a cough reflex and the foreign object can be coughed out. We knew this as it had happened once or twice before. But nothing was helping.

"The ambulance arrived and we were taken to Alder Hey, where she was examined and x-rayed, but nothing showed up. However, Rebecca was still in quite a bit of discomfort so she was admitted to a ward for observation. As the day progressed, we realised that she wasn't herself, and by the evening she had a bad headache which she couldn't get rid of. The following morning, a doctor came to see us and said we could go home. I questioned the fact that her headache had remained throughout the night, but he said some fresh air would probably cure it. He left the room and I helped Rebecca out of bed to dress her. I turned to find her clothes and when I turned back again Rebecca had gone blue and was like a rag doll. I pressed the emergency button and everyone appeared. They started to work on Rebecca and within moments she had regained her colour and we were on our way to x-ray. A couple of hours later, Rebecca was taken to theatre to have the piece of apple removed from the top of her left lung!

"During her recovery from the operation that afternoon she became very unwell again because her lung had collapsed. The medical staff carried out the necessary treatment and she looked to have turned the corner. But the next day the staff on the ward were unhappy with her progress so the ICU consultant was called in. He worked his magic on her but decided she should be taken to ICU as a precaution. Rebecca, however, made a speedy recovery and was discharged after a few days - but she never ate an apple again!"

Such was her tenacity that within a few days she was on the team bus heading for Blackpool. It was a memorable occasion for her and the other youngsters with T shirts being presented with 'North West' printed on them, and each team member also had a shirt with their name emblazoned on the back. Even the judges were dressed appropriately in navy and white. Rules were strict, too, and any youngster whose wheelchair inadvertently crossed a line suffered disqualification.

Rebecca was entered in three events, being a late entrant in one sport she was not familiar with, so wasn't placed. The ramp ball event was completed early on but the result was not announced until later in the day. Her mum, in her capacity as carer and team supporter, anxiously waited for the outcome.

Said Sue: "Rebecca had done quite well but we didn't know everyone else's score. She was also waiting to take part in her third event, which was going to be the last of the day. We were sitting having our lunch, enjoying the day and watching the other children, when the announcement came over the loudspeaker informing us of the bronze and silver winners in the girls' under-13 ramp ball, and then telling us Rebecca Pye had won the gold.

"The whole place erupted. I was speechless. Rebecca hadn't got a clue what was going on - she was cheering along with everybody else but didn't know why she was cheering - but I was just delighted to realise my daughter had got a gold medal and she was competing against the rest of the country. It was just amazing. I phoned Nick and told him that his daughter was a gold medal winner and a champion of Britain. He thought I was joking at first.

"When I got home I asked him if he had told anyone and he said he had rung my mother and father, and said no more, but when we got to church the following morning everyone knew, so he must have rung many more. Rebecca also won a silver in the precision bean bag. So a gold and a silver on her first attempt wasn't bad. She was delighted, but mainly because we were so delighted in what she had achieved. So it was a good finish to her first year at Sandfield."

The impression among the staff at the open evenings was that Rebecca had made good progress. She retained her healthy dislike for maths despite the encouragement from her teacher, but PHSE (life skills) which dealt with subjects like shopping and personal hygiene, was a subject she loved. Rebecca, of course, always enjoyed baking with mum at home and she was an enthusiastic pupil when it came to cookery classes. She was not slow, either, in telling her teacher she was doing things wrong in the kitchen (she and her mum prepared and cooked in a different way) but the teacher saw the funny side of the criticism!

Science and experiments, albeit in very simple terms, and discussions about the human body also interested her. The times she spent in hospital gave her something of an insight into the subject and she was able to use that knowledge in her school work. Again, so simplistic for most people, but for Rebecca it was an achievement.

There was no doubt she had thrived at Sandfield in her first year and her achievements gave her confidence. She didn't make friends easily, but this was a legacy of her days at Childwall when she rarely needed to instigate a conversation because people would come and talk to her.

Despite the turmoil of changing schools, and taking her time to settle into her new surroundings, Rebecca soon grasped the opportunities that were presented - a tribute to the doctrine and approach to pupils at Sandfield, as much as her easy going nature.

School head John Hudson believed that her personality played a tremendous part in the way she adapted to the change.

"It was strange for Rebecca moving from a mainstream primary with larger numbers of children, but it didn't seem to faze her. She quickly established herself within the school. She perhaps was used to being the star and children would help, but she was remarkably independent and very skilled at ensuring she achieved what she wanted to achieve. You encouraged her to have a go.

"She got to know virtually everybody right away, and I am sure many people have talked about Rebecca's smile. I have always said that if I could have bottled her smile I would have made a fortune. Every morning when you saw her and said 'hello' she would look at you and then a wonderful beam would come across her face.

"Rebecca had a great strength of will and a determination - it was that determination that had pulled her through so many things in the past. She would be in hospital, then out of intensive care and within a day or two would be back in school. She bounced back like a rubber ball and that resilience came through. She liked music and being in on conversations. It's a great quality in life that you have an interest in what goes on about you, and that is what she had. There was a lot of adult conversation around her and she would love to earwig on what was happening. But she was also caring towards others within her group and she would notice if any other members of the class were upset and she would respond to that."

As a school, Sandfield specialises in working with many children suffering varying degrees of disability. There had been instances when pupils had died, Mr Hudson reflected, but he emphasised the importance of providing an expansive programme for pupils to bring the best out of them.

"It's at the back of your mind but you can't allow it to take over otherwise you will be denying opportunities to the young people concerned. You look to make the experience as rich as possible, so they get their full entitlement to education and their full entitlement to all those life-enriching activities. I know it is a bit of a cliché but some people manage to pack into a few short years more than some people who live an awful lot longer. We still follow the national curriculum and all the entitlement that goes with that is still implicit in what we do. But whenever opportunities do come to enrich that curriculum, to exploit opportunities, we take them."

Smaller class groups - they are no bigger than seven or nine pupils and at least two members of staff - offer a great advantage, while staff, he said, are always open to new ideas and provide additional activities outside normal school hours.

Mr Hudson stressed that while discipline was maintained it was vital that pupils showed spirit, and that certainly was one of Rebecca's many attributes. "If she was told off she would be downcast for a few seconds. You might get a 'sorry' from her and then it was over. She never went away and sulked. Overall, the thing that affected everyone was her determination, her love and zest for life, and taking part in everything. Even on days when she can't have been feeling well and it was difficult for her, she still took part in things and she wasn't going to let the medical issues get in the way of what she wanted to achieve. She overcame problems and through all she did that wonderful smile would be there."

Being part of the athletics set-up and becoming involved in a team environment helped to develop Rebecca's love for sport and gave her a sense of accomplishment.

"She loved being part of the team," stated Sue Barry, PE co-ordinator, who took Rebecca for sport and RE. "The first time we travelled to Manchester for the trials I assumed wrongly that Rebecca would go with Sue in their van. But Sue asked if she could go on the team bus because she wanted to be part of the team. That was lovely and a big thing for her and you get a great buzz from that. The winning doesn't really matter, but if you win it's a wonderful feeling and she was a part of that. She loved her medals, loved her trophies, and we had great support from Sue and Jane.

"Jane was wonderful with her and when I first had Rebecca in lessons I would take my lead from Jane as to what Rebecca could do. Jane was very good in motivating her and encouraging her. She really loved PE and gave her all, but the ones that stand out are the gymnastics and the dance lessons because she really responded to music. To see her out of her chair was wonderful. She was very flexible with her legs and body and was very good on the soft play apparatus.

"In the athletics you look at the child, look at their ability and see what event they would be best suited for. It follows from there. Overawed is not a word I would use to describe Rebecca. She revelled in the competition, was a very sociable child and just enjoyed the fun side of things because sport can bring so much fun. As a pupil, there was always the smile, the enthusiasm, the sense of fun, a little bit of naughtiness, but that's great as it was part of her character."

Rebecca, who had just turned twelve, continued to thrive in her second year and achieved further success in sport - but, sadly, in the face of periods when she was feeling anything but well. In fact, it seemed that the effects of Leigh Syndrome were causing her more stress than had recently been the case, and it appeared that the traumatic times of the past for her parents might be returning.

Chapter Twelve

Agonising Decision

SOME decisions you have to make in life are easy; some are more difficult. And then there are the impossible ones.

In the eight years since Rebecca was diagnosed with Leigh Syndrome, Sue and Nick had made innumerable decisions, with so many of them based on what was best for their daughter in the light of her life-threatening illness.

They had given her all the love, all the care, all the support they possibly could, and many of those decisions, sometimes taken under duress, had helped to enrich her life.

Their lives had been turned upside down from the moment Rebecca became seriously ill. They had been through the most emotional of times with the uncertainty surrounding her condition and the fact that their daughter had been so close to death on numerous occasions.

But constantly nagging at the back of their minds was the thought that their brave little girl may eventually be overwhelmed by the disease - and when that time came they would have to make the most difficult decision any parents had to face.

There were only six pupils in her class at the start of her second year at Sandfield so Rebecca benefited from the individual attention she received. She enjoyed going to school with Jane, enjoyed the classroom atmosphere and the camaraderie with her classmates. Occasionally, there would be homework, but it was often a struggle as her concentration levels were generally poor, and mum had to cajole and help her.

It was a case of doing things at her own pace. No-one was going to change that and her mum believed it was this approach that fashioned the type of character she became.

"I don't think some people realised she had her own thoughts and ideas," said Sue. "She couldn't communicate that well, but could make herself understood to me and Nick and those close to her, yet she did have her own ideas and would tell me. She would say the most funny things, which you would repeat to others. I am quite convinced they thought we had made them up because when she was with people she wasn't so sure of she didn't speak, or would only speak when she was spoken to, because people didn't always have the time to listen. But that is every day life and how the world is, but it was a shame people sometimes didn't have the time because they would have got a lot more out of her."

Rebecca took part in the school assemblies and the Christmas production. Sandfield offered opportunities for their pupils to join several clubs but she preferred her sport and as 2008 dawned she could look ahead to the lighter nights when the athletics started again.

The trials for selection to the North West team were held in Manchester again and although she didn't do as well as the previous year Rebecca gained enough points to earn her place, and win two bronze medals into the bargain. The prospect of another trip to Blackpool was an exciting one, and her mum came up with a unique way of preparing for one of the events.

"We got our friendly roof man to cut off a piece of guttering and my dad put a wooden handle on it so Rebecca could practise her ramp ball," said Sue. "You had to roll a heavy ball down the tubing or, in our case the guttering, aiming for a target, with the larger numbers further away. So there was a skill in angling the equipment and the speed you rolled the ball. In competition, the person holding the bottom of the ramp is not allowed to see the target so it was up to Rebecca to tell you where to move the target. It was a case of working together on that.

"We would go out to the front of our house, and we would mark out on the paving obstacles that she could aim for and we practised most mornings while we waited for the taxi to come to take Rebecca to school. On other days we would be throwing bean bags, so anyone driving or walking past must have thought we were totally mad."

During this time, though, Rebecca had become lethargic and had spells when she was unwell. The effects of her condition were obviously bubbling under the surface, not necessarily sufficient to raise alarms, but worrying enough. Her parents had booked a holiday to Benalmadena in mainland Spain for the May half term and hoped the sunshine would prove beneficial to her. But she was poorly on the flight there and back, resulting in several visits to Alder Hey to discuss the situation with doctors.

"It had started in May," Sue went on, "and she had become very tired and everything was becoming an effort for her. On the flight out on holiday her oxygen levels were not very good. As soon as we came down from altitude she improved but while she seemed okay on holiday we were still concerned.

"The flight home was awful. It was a late night flight, she was very tired and fell asleep, which didn't help because her oxygen levels were suppressed even more. The last hour of the flight, in particular, was terrible. She was struggling and had a bad headache, due to the lack of oxygen. As soon as we got back down into Manchester she said her headache was better and, while she was nowhere near her normal self, she had improved."

Her parents discussed their experiences with the medical profession on their return. Sue spoke at length to an Alder Hey doctor by phone and he said he would consult with a colleague before meeting them. He rang back suggesting they take Rebecca in for tests. In fact, she ended up in hospital anyway, apparently with a chest infection. The couple also met with Dr Andrew Morris, who had originally confirmed the diagnosis in October 2000 and whom they had seen on an annual basis in Newcastle since, to discuss the symptoms and what might be happening.

Said Sue: "I received a phone call from school saying Rebecca's oxygen levels were poor. She was grey when I saw her and immediately thought that she should go to hospital. They kept her in because they couldn't keep her oxygen levels up. They thought she had an infection, but when they took some samples nothing came back to confirm it, so we were discharged two days later. It was a Friday morning, but by Friday afternoon I was back in A&E because she was quite poorly.

"I had taken her home and she wouldn't eat her lunch and was just like a rag doll again. Rebecca was put back on a ward but it was uncertain as to what was wrong with her. She spent four or five days there and we were eventually discharged because there were no clear-cut answers, although she looked a little bit better. We carried on, but Nick and I were not sure. We just had this horrible feeling things weren't right.

"The consultant (neurological) asked us to bring her in for more tests and we saw him at the end of June. Rebecca had a couple of blood tests and I knew she wasn't well because she just sat there and let them take the blood, which wasn't like her."

Irrespective of how well prepared one might be to receive bad news it always comes as a shock. What followed confirmed the couple's worst fears - words they were hoping they would never hear.

Sue continued: "We went in to see the consultant, along with the ICU consultant, and they said things were not good at all. Luckily, we had taken Jane with us that day, and at this point she and Rebecca left the room. We had a long talk with both of them and they said it was time to make a decision as to what we were going to do.

"It was a stark assessment but we had asked them to be honest all along. We felt there was no point in pussy-footing around. We needed to know what was going on so we could make an informed decision. We knew things had taken a turn for the worse, but they had done on so many other occasions. However, this time we were told that if Rebecca went in to ICU, which they said is what they recommended on medical grounds, she would be sedated, put on a ventilator and wouldn't come off it again. They said that this time the amount of carbon dioxide in her bloodstream was so great that they were surprised that she was coping as she was. She had 72 per cent carbon dioxide in her blood and just 28 per cent oxygen.

"So it was a case of what to do then.

"Nick and I had made the decision that when the time came we wouldn't commit Rebecca to a ventilator permanently. It certainly wasn't an easy decision to make, but both of us felt that you live life to the full while you have got it, and you can't prolong something where there would be no quality of life at all. Also, we were asking ourselves what Rebecca would want - that was our main concern. Would she want to be in a hospital and on a ventilator indefinitely, unable to do anything for herself? Even if she was able to sit in a wheelchair being on a ventilator was so limiting, and she would just be absolutely mad with that."

They knew, too, that the choice of ventilation would result in having to make another decision, even greater and more heart-rending further down the line, and that was when the machine would have to be switched off. They considered the consequences of that, the emotional stress involved, and how they might come to terms with determining effectively when to end their daughter's life. They were aware that any decision they made would only be in Rebecca's best interests, but finally it would be theirs, anyway. So they informed the consultants that they we were going to take Rebecca home.

"They fully agreed with our decision," stated Sue, "and I always remember one of the consultants asking me if we appreciated that Rebecca might die that coming weekend. I just turned to him and said that was silly, she couldn't, because it was her birthday party that weekend. I felt he must have thought I was totally and utterly mad and possibly thinking 'you stupid woman, this child is dying and you are talking about her birthday party!'

"We went home and Nick went back to work, although he hardly wanted to, and as it was Friday I set about preparing for Rebecca's party on the Sunday, even though her birthday was actually on the Monday."

Sunday, June 29, arrived. Family and friends had been informed about the party well in advance. Sue and Nick could have called it off at a late stage, but they thought that if she saw those she loved it may be something of a tonic for Rebecca. But it was surreal. People arrived with all sorts of presents, Sue had prepared an excellent buffet, the couple put on a brave face in what must have been a distressing time, while the star of the show herself was feeling decidedly unwell.

"I don't quite know how Nick and I got through it," Sue admitted. "This was her last party. We didn't want to tell anyone. What do you say to people: 'Welcome. This may be the last time you will see Rebecca!' But we did get through it. Rebecca wasn't really up to having the party. She was struggling, but on the Monday she took a cake in to school.

"The doctor had said he would see us on the following Wednesday but rang to re-arrange it for the Friday. I said 'okay, and by the way, Rebecca turned 13 and was at school'. He must have thought I was cruel, but what do you do? Things had to go on as normally as possible for her.

"We saw the doctor on the Friday - Rebecca didn't come with us - and we talked about palliative care. He informed us they were going to take that route and put us in touch with the Macmillan nurses. They said arrangements wouldn't be in place by the weekend so they needed to give us some advice as to what to do in case anything happened. I told him that Rebecca was going off to Blackpool the following day to compete in the National Disabled Games, so nothing was going to happen that weekend."

It was a courageous decision. Rebecca had been looking forward to being part of the team. She wanted the chance to compete, to possibly win a medal or two, but in truth she wasn't really well enough. However, nothing could douse her spirit!

"Rebecca wanted to go and I wasn't going to stop her," said Sue. "We took the oxygen with us. It was a very wet day and she competed in her ramp ball and target bean bag events, winning a bronze and a silver, and we then returned home. It was a two-day event but I told her PE teacher that there was no way we could manage the next day as Rebecca wasn't up to it.

"Rebecca rested the next day, which was unlike her, and we just pottered around. It was strange, and looking back you do wonder, but she asked me if I would take a photograph of her. I took some photographs and set the camera up on the table for photos of the two of us together."

In typically resolute fashion, Rebecca went to school that week, during which the palliative care team visited Sue to start setting things in motion. These were incredibly trying circumstances. Nick still had the burden of work, but with more urgent family matters on his mind, while Sue tried to carry on as if life was normal. It was anything but. Their whole world was crashing down around them. They shared their anguish with a few members of the family and a very few close friends whom they had taken into their confidence and who were all extremely supportive to them. But nobody else was aware of the crisis.

The uncertainty of it all added to the distress. Their decisions had been made. Time was running out, but when would the end come, if this really was the end?

Chapter Thirteen

A Peaceful End

IT was school sports day on the Friday and nothing was going to stop Rebecca from taking part - not even the palliative care doctor who arrived that morning at Sandfield to assess her condition.

Staff were aware that her illness was becoming more debilitating, but not to the extent that it actually was, and yet Rebecca, showing her usual stoicism, completed her events.

That night, the family drove to Wales, having planned a weekend at a cottage with Nick's sister, Jacqui, and her family. Rebecca didn't have a good night, due to the fact that her oxygen levels were so poor, but by morning she was more alert.

Sue recalled: "I remember sitting on her bed, just the two of us because it was still fairly early, but fully light. We were looking out of the window and Rebecca commented on the beautiful scenery. Normally, she didn't bother saying things like that, but we spoke about the landscape. You don't think at the time 'why has she said that?'"

Everyone was looking forward to the trip that day to Bodnant Gardens. It was summer, but typically chilly, yet worries about the weather became insignificant when fears over Rebecca's health increased. All the energy appeared to drain from her when her mum was changing her clothes in the car and she could not get her up off the seat. Suddenly, there was an urgency to get her back to Liverpool, and it became an uncomfortable journey for her even with the help of oxygen.

On arrival home, Rebecca was suffering from a headache and Sue contacted the Macmillan nurses who advised medication. Her daughter was very agitated after being put to bed in the early evening so the palliative care doctor was phoned. She suggested ringing the GP, who wasn't working that night, but the worried parents were put through to an on-call doctor who arrived later. He informed the palliative care doctor by phone of the situation and a Macmillan nurse visited to give Rebecca some medication to calm her. It was just after midnight and she did settle, but the nurse delivered a shock assessment to Sue and Nick, suggesting they sat with their daughter because it was unlikely she would survive the night. The realisation that their daughter was facing a last desperate battle was both heartbreaking and mind-numbing, but her parents remained incredibly strong. They had to - there was no choice. And Rebecca bravely held on during the night.

"We were cheered by the fact that we had got through Saturday night and Sunday morning, although we did think she would wake up and she would be fine again," admitted Sue. "I suppose we knew deep within ourselves that this would not happen. When daylight came we thought we had better start letting people know what was happening. We phoned our friends, David and Jennie, who very kindly came round and sat with Rebecca while we freshened up, and we called my mum and dad and my brothers, Don and Dave. Rebecca was in and out of consciousness. When mum and dad arrived my dad wanted to make himself useful so I sent him to buy some biscuits and cake in case anyone wanted something to eat. Mum sat with Rebecca for a little while.

"She started to wake up a bit but was obviously extremely weak, and I gave her a wash and put her in fresh pyjamas, brushed her hair and tried to make her more comfortable. The community nurse called just to let us know they were there to give us whatever support we needed. By early afternoon the news had spread and friends and family knew that Rebecca wasn't well at home. People arrived all day long. Both Nick and I felt we weren't there, but just floating, which sounds strange, but if I had the time over again and asked myself about whether I would have done it differently the answer would have been 'no'. Rebecca saw the people she loved because that is what she wanted."

Distressing though the situation appeared, and with any hope seemingly futile, Rebecca still found the strength to suggest all was not lost.

"We were buoyed a little bit because she did ask for something to eat," said Nick. "Rebecca was very fond of her food and we took this in the beginning as a good sign. It was only a small amount, some milk shake and a bit of yoghurt, but it gave us a lift.

"Claire House had been in touch after speaking to the Macmillan team and told us they had started an initiative of care at home, so they could send someone over to look after Rebecca on the Sunday night. We were extremely grateful for that because we had been looking after Rebecca as best we could from the drive back from Wales on the Saturday all the way through the Sunday. The thought that there was somebody qualified to sit with her while we were only across the landing was very comforting for us. Lesley, from Claire House, arrived around 8.00pm and Rebecca was asleep.

"We were feeling slightly better about things because we didn't expect from what we had been told that Rebecca would have lasted through the day," Nick went on. "We were thinking that it could just be that once more she might turn the corner and fool everyone. So probably on the Sunday night our spirits were a little bit higher. The emotion of it had been all-engulfing as well as physically exhausting, so we just crashed out. We felt that in order to be able to do our best on the Monday we needed to get some sort of rest."

Exhaustion was inevitable. Sue and Nick had experienced it so many times before during Rebecca's rollercoaster of illness. It may be easy to adopt an auto pilot mentality, but sooner or later the strain takes its toll. They tried to sleep, having told Lesley to wake them if anything untoward happened, but Sue knew she had to be up by 6.00am anyway because Lesley was travelling back to her home in Wales.

"Although we had carers on numerous occasions, it felt wrong to be lying in bed knowing how ill Rebecca was and somebody else was looking after her," said Sue. "That is what really made up my mind that I was definitely going to spend Monday night with her and care for her myself.

"On the Monday morning I walked into the room hoping Rebecca would be sitting up. She wasn't. I was thinking that if she was going to turn the corner she would have done so by now. Lesley left and I made a cup of tea, the first of the day, and then I sat with Rebecca believing she would wake up in a few minutes. I put her television on. It was a ritual that as soon as Rebecca woke up the television went on and I wondered if the sound of the programmes she enjoyed would awaken her. But they didn't. She seemed fairly comfortable, but her colour was poor. She was pallid and her lips were a mauve colour - a sign that there was a lack of oxygen and she was not getting rid of the carbon dioxide, which was the great problem.

"There was an offer of a carer from Claire House and Alder Hey on the Monday night. I thanked them for their offers but declined. I wanted to do it myself. I spoke to Nick about it and he was happy with that. I am a strong-willed person, it was my child and I wanted to be there to say 'good morning, have you had a good night's sleep'. But it wasn't to be."

Jane Young arrived, coincidentally with Tony, the taxi driver, who had called to take Rebecca to school. She told him that Rebecca was poorly. Sue and Jane then sat with Rebecca, who had woken up. They talked to her, occasionally receiving 'yes' and 'no' answers, and they tried to make her smile, succeeding in small ways. Meanwhile, Nick informed his office he would not be going in to work, and then went shopping as there was little food in the house after being away in Wales.

Jane helped Sue to change Rebecca's bedding and give her a bed bath. During this they noticed a small bedsore so Sue rang the community nurse for advise. She was told not to do anything until they arrived.

"I told them there was no need," said Sue, "but they said they were on their way. I suppose, in a way, I should have started to think 'Why?', but two of them came and it took three of us to turn Rebecca so they could tend to the bedsore, which was only very small. They decided there and then that she needed a different mattress and immediately ordered one. I thought to myself that it would take a couple of days for it to arrive so obviously they thought things were okay, but I had a phone call an hour after they left to say the mattress would be delivered that afternoon! The nurses said they would call back later, which I thought was very strange, given it was only a bedsore."

It was a hot afternoon, the sun was shining directly into Rebecca's room, and trying to keep it cool was difficult. It wasn't helped by the fact that when Dr Linda Brook, the palliative care consultant, arrived there were nine in the room - the doctor and her assistant, a couple of Macmillan nurses, Jan Rowlands, the community nurse, Jane, Rebecca and her mum and dad.

"The doctor felt one of three possible scenarios might occur," said Nick. "One was that Rebecca might have a pulmonary embolism, and she described two other conditions which might arise, both of which, she told us gently, would cause Rebecca to pass away. I said 'what could we do?' and I suppose I was questioning in my own mind whether our decision was the right one. But we had gone down the palliative route and I told the doctor that this is what we had decided because we wanted to make sure Rebecca would not suffer, be uncomfortable or be distressed. If we could give her the best chance possible by keeping her calm and free from distress and pain and let nature overcome the problems she had that was surely the kindest way it could happen, and if that was not to be we could do no more.

"My thoughts went back to what one of the Macmillan nurses had said on the Saturday night when the stark reality of what was happening was hitting home to us. We had questioned then whether we should change our minds and take her to hospital and put her on a ventilator and subject her to that indignity, discomfort, pain and unpleasantness, but the nurse had asked us who would we be doing it for, her best interests or our own? She was right.

"We wanted Rebecca to be as calm, serene and as peaceful as possible, without pain. She had defied the medics before and we were thinking she might do it again, but the doctor left us in no doubt that wasn't going to be the case this time."

Stressful as it was to accept, the couple acknowledged the fact that the signs this time compared to her other major setbacks were different. She wasn't going to pull through, although they knew it would be wrong to give up believing that a miracle might happen. But if Rebecca was going to die, it would be on her terms. She was a determined young lady who had hung on all weekend and it appeared she would only give up her battle for life after seeing the family and friends she loved. They included her grandparents, who had been waiting for news downstairs. After Sue told them what the doctor had said they went up to see her for a few minutes. Sue's father quietly told Rebecca she was his little villain, to which she responded, 'yes, I am your big villain'.

The school had been notified about Rebecca's condition and she was visited by her teacher, Mr Williams, who brought along the medal she had so gallantly won just three days before on the sports day despite being poorly.

"Rebecca's face lit up because she was pleased to see him," said her mum. "He chatted for a few minutes and then presented her with the medal. She raised her head ever so slightly so that he could put it over her. He said to her that he had better go and that he would see her next term. She mouthed 'next term' and then she puckered up for a kiss. He looked at us to seek our consent and I said it was fine, so he gave her a kiss and she looked so delighted. After Mr Williams had gone the mattress arrived. It took 20 minutes to inflate, during which time I used the hoist to lift Rebecca out of bed and put her in new pyjamas to make her as comfortable as possible. But tiredness was etched on her face. She was exhausted from the physical effort of being lifted, changed and having to sit down. Her colour was also horrendous, as it had been for so long."

Dr Brook had left medication for Rebecca, whose organs, her parents were told, had started to cease functioning, as was usual in such situations.

"I shouted down to Nick at that point, asking him if he was going to help. He informed me that someone else had arrived to see Rebecca. I thought 'oh no, there's me berating Nick for sitting downstairs', but I was unaware Rebecca's PE teacher, Sue Barry, had arrived. She had crossed paths with the mattress man so hadn't rung the bell. We had a bit of a laugh about that later! You have to have a small joke sometimes regardless of the situation.

"She came up but the mattress was still inflating. Rebecca was in a chair - we had propped her up - but she couldn't sit up straight. Sue stayed for 20 minutes and we eventually put Rebecca back into bed. She dropped off to sleep straightaway. She was totally exhausted and the relief of being able to lie down was plain to see. We had a bit of a lull after that from visitors, for which I was so grateful because although they were so welcome Rebecca needed a rest."

When Nick's sister arrived later she had not seen Rebecca since the Saturday in Wales. Sue and Nick had told them to stay on at the cottage, but they had travelled up to Liverpool on Monday. She was on her own - her husband, John, was looking after the children - and she was obviously very concerned at her niece's condition. She sat with her reading Noddy stories which Rebecca always enjoyed. Other callers included Barbara and Ian, who had been away at the URC General Assembly in Edinburgh, Jennie and David and Marianne.

"There was always a chair in Rebecca's room for her carer, and we had taken another one upstairs to use. Barbara and Jacqui were sitting on them and I said it wasn't fair that I was standing. Rebecca just patted her bed and I got on with her. It was most uncomfortable because it was a water bed, but I just lay there with her and she put her arm around me. We quite often did that and I used to joke with her when she got into bed that I would climb in, say goodnight, and go to sleep. She would push me to get me out, saying it was her bed and to leave her alone, but on this occasion we had a cuddle, until I had to stand up due to the bed being too uncomfortable for me, although it was relieving the pressure on Rebecca. But I was so very glad I had that cuddle."

It was a pleasant surprise when the minister, the Rev Gordon Smith, turned up as he had only just arrived back from Edinburgh, too. He went up to see Rebecca and told her everyone was praying for her. She quietly replied that she knew.

Her faith throughout her young life had been simplistic. She believed that there was good in everybody, and believed in Jesus. She had decided after attending a couple of Confirmation classes at Allerton URC that she didn't want to be Confirmed. Her parents told her she would have to tell Gordon, so she did, but when he asked her why she wasn't able to tell him. However, he told her that all he wanted her to do was to tell him that Jesus loved her. She had replied "oh, I know He does." And the minister said that was all Rebecca needed to tell him at the special Sunday service. She said she could do that. The Confirmation had only taken place in May - just a couple of months previously

"I think that when Gordon told her everyone was praying for her and she had replied, I think she felt that was okay," said her mum. "She may have thought she had seen all those she needed to see, and the people whom she hadn't would understand. So she could go now. But it wasn't the right time for us."

The last of the visitors went at 10.20pm. Sue had worked out the times of her medicines, had settled Rebecca down and put a story tape on for her. She then sorted out the put-you-up bed for herself and Nick joined her to say goodnight to Rebecca. They still both maintained a slender hope that she might survive.

Sue managed a fitful sleep for a short time, but remained conscious to her daughter's every movement and word.

"It was one of those sleeps like when you are on the beach and drift off, but you can hear everything and you are aware of your surroundings. Your body is resting but your mind is very much alert. She needed medication at 2.00am and I programmed my mind to do that. I knew she was still with us because the medication was a relaxant for her and had to be rubbed on her gum right at the back because apparently it absorbs into the bloodstream quicker. Putting your finger in Rebecca's mouth was a risky business at any time, and she clenched her teeth because she didn't like the taste, didn't want it and moved her head. I told her it would make her a bit calmer and help her to have a good sleep.

"She looked as if she was in the most uncomfortable position - her legs were crossed - but we knew that was her favourite position. One arm was up over her pillow and the other was down the side of the bed. It was the way she always slept. I sat and read and popped down to make a cup of tea. I drank the tea and flipped through the magazines. I thought I would just check on her and if she was okay I would lie down again. I went over and she had gone. I heard nothing. She was so peaceful. I just said 'Rebecca'. I touched her and she wasn't warm. I pulled the cover over her and kept repeating 'Rebecca, Rebecca'. There was no response so I ran across the landing to Nick."

It was a few minutes before five o'clock. It was the middle of July so the day was breaking and it was semi-light.

Nick said: "I had been asleep for about three hours. I jumped straight out of bed because I couldn't believe what Sue was telling me. But she had gone. There was no sign of any breathing. It was as though she had just gone to sleep. There was no sign of any distress or discomfort. We talked to her and just tried to make sense of it. We kept talking to her in case for some reason she was still able to hear what we were saying, although we really knew she couldn't. We kept talking to her, stroking her hair for 20 minutes looking for a sign of life, but there was none."

Despite their grief they were aware that people had to be contacted - the Macmillan nurse on call and Sue's brother, Don, a nurse, whom they asked to call over to confirm that Rebecca had died even though they knew that her courageous struggle was over. He stayed with them for a while, during which time the Macmillan nurse, along with community nurses Jan and Sandra, arrived. Being fully appreciative of the circumstances they remained calm and gentle, prepared to do anything Sue and Nick asked of them.

After all they had gone through it would have been both easy and acceptable for them to have fallen apart, to let the pent-up emotions of the nightmare scenario they had faced over many years pour out in what was so sorrowful a time, but Rebecca would not have wanted them to do that. In the back of their minds they knew that, despite their world now completely shattered, procedures still had to be adhered to, particularly through the complication of Rebecca's passing at home.

Jan Rowlands rang the out-of-hours doctors because a GP had to certify the death. The certificate, however, could only be signed by Dr Brook, as she was the last doctor to examine Rebecca.

"It was very important that the course of action we had decided to take - the palliative route - was properly documented because of the situation where you have a death at home in such circumstances," stated Nick. "We were told that if the palliative care procedure was not followed correctly enquiries could be made perhaps by police officers. That was the last thing we needed. However, the on-call doctor came out and examined Rebecca and confirmed there were no signs of life, and he left some paperwork for us."

Sue didn't feel ready to return to Rebecca's bedroom with Jan and Sandra, who wanted to help straighten Rebecca's bed. They went up, tidied her hair and put clean pyjamas on her, adding some lip gloss because Rebecca's lips were very dry. Before they left they made several calls, including ones to the hospital and Sandfield Park, where Sue Barry took the call.

Sue and Nick phoned David and Jennie, who rushed round straightaway, and they also contacted Dave, Sue's other brother. Nick rang his sister, who was very distressed at the news; Jane (Young) was called - she was too overcome to reply and put the phone down; Debbie, the secretary at Childwall, who had been one of the people who had trained to look after Rebecca at lunch times, was also told. She said she would inform Mrs Shaw, Rebecca's former head. Sue spoke to her friend, Dot, and Nick rang his office.

Within minutes, it seemed, the house was crowded.

"In some ways it just felt so wrong that so many people had called and the person who would have loved to have been at the centre of things with the people she loved wasn't," said Sue. "But we put on a brave face because that is what Rebecca would have wanted.

"I don't know how many cups of tea I made. It was something to do while Nick was talking to people. Don left and very kindly said he would go and break the news to my mum and dad. There was no way I could have spoken to them on the phone, and it wasn't the way that they should find out, anyway. They came later on in the morning after Don and Delyth and Jane, my sisters-in-law, had visited them because they had lost their granddaughter.

"When my mum and dad arrived mum threw me out of the kitchen, telling me that was her place. They didn't know what to say to us, and we didn't know what to say to them. People drifted away, others arrived, including my brother, Dave, Jane and Debbie, who was in a dreadful state. Jane was holding it together, just.

"When Jan came back mid-morning she said she would just go up to see Rebecca. She came back down and told us Rebecca was now smiling. I know it is a physical thing that happens, with muscles relaxing, but we went up and she had a little semblance of a smile. Jane went up to see her and came running down saying 'she's smiling at me'. I said 'but she always did, Jane, didn't she'. This set Debbie and Jane off. Then the people from the funeral service arrived at lunchtime to collect Rebecca.

By this time people had started to slip away, leaving Sue and Nick on their own to reflect on the immediate past heartbreaking events.

"David and Jennie came back in the early evening to 'field' the phone calls, while we spoke to the funeral director, Alan Hughes, and our minister," commented Nick. "There were so many calls, including one from the minister who was at our church when Rebecca first came to us. People were trying to hold out their hands in support and wanted to show they cared. In a way it was actually a comfort talking to people. Trying to put any sense together to make decisions about the funeral service was difficult. It wasn't even 24 hours and we were being asked to make such decisions, but there wasn't any pressure put on us at all. Alan was extremely efficient and kind and just wanted to do his best for us and guide us through. You do these things on auto pilot. Perhaps it's something logical to concentrate on after the most traumatic of events."

It all seemed surreal for the pair as talk switched from hymns they might want, to the type of coffin and then the flowers - all part of the 'procedure'.

The day flew by in some respects, dragged in others. Sue and Nick had had little sleep and they were in need of rest after everyone had left and the house had become quiet. But it was hardly the environment they had been used to down the years, as Sue recalled: "It was very strange; there was no-one to listen out for, and the house was so empty. There were the two of us in it, of course, but it was dreadfully empty.

"Although Rebecca had spent many nights in hospital, we knew she was coming back. I would go in her room when she was in hospital, tidy her bed, stupidly talk to her toys to say Rebecca would be back soon. Just something. But this time there was nothing to do - she would not be coming back."

Chapter Fourteen

Our Final Farewell

DEATH brings with it desolation. The feeling of loss is incomparable; the pain inescapable; the despair inconceivable.

Sue and Nick's lives were suddenly and unbearably thrust into darkness. For almost 13 years Rebecca had been their focus, their love, their care, their joy and their sorrow. Their feelings now were of a vast emptiness.

They knew it had been coming; they knew that the disease would finally overwhelm her; but even an awareness of the inevitable fails to prepare you for the grief that follows.

To lose any loved one is heartbreaking enough. When it is your only child the shock is exacerbated. Devastating.

Sue and Nick looked to each other for support and strength, as they attempted to make sense of their tragedy. They gained some comfort, too, as family and friends rallied round.

But dealing with bereavement, particularly with one so young who epitomised the very meaning of life, is an individualistic matter.

"I couldn't go into Rebecca's room for a few days," admitted Sue. "I got up early and I ironed. It was something to do because all of a sudden I had absolutely nothing to do."

Nick, however, did go into her room "as a way of communicating with her," but recalled the strangeness of it all in the days immediately after

Rebecca's death. "To go from spending every waking moment looking after a person to having nothing to do was weird. I felt it was weird enough and I spent a lot of my time working, so how Sue must have felt I just don't know. We didn't have too long on the Wednesday to dwell on things because from quite an early time there were letters being put through the door and phone calls."

One of the first letters received was hand delivered from one of Nick's clients. The businessman hadn't met Rebecca, but had heard the news and wanted to express his feelings. More sympathy cards arrived, and callers. They included two of Nick's partners from the office, the head of Childwall C of E, and two friends who brought food which was most welcome as cooking was the last thing on their minds.

On the Wednesday afternoon, Sue and Nick met up with Jacqui, John and their children, Matthew and Lydia, at Calderstones Park. It was the first time they had seen their nephew and niece since the weekend in Wales.

"Matthew came straight up to me and said how sorry he was about Rebecca," said Nick. "Then, to bring us back down to earth later we got back to the car and found one of the tyres was completely flat. We just laughed and said that that was because Rebecca wanted to be at the park with us."

Thursday was a bleak day. The couple registered Rebecca's death in Liverpool city centre and the weather added to the gloom as the rain bounced off the pavements with considerable force. After seeing Sue's mum and dad to keep them informed they received a visit from Sandfield's head of governors, before going to visit friends for a meal.

The funeral date was set for the following Tuesday, July 22 - exactly a week after Rebecca died. There had been frustrations over the delay in securing the death certificate before finalising funeral arrangements and then making plans to visit Rebecca at the Chapel of Rest on the Friday.

"I didn't know that I wanted to go," stated Sue. "Nick was adamant that he was going. I think it was just the way I had been brought up that once someone had gone you remember them as they were. But this was very different, and I was so glad that I went. We chatted to her and we took Barney, her constant companion, and left him with her."

Being alone with Rebecca was a comfort. The days immediately after her death had been hectic, with comings and goings at home, or the visits to complete necessary official business, see family or have a meal with friends. Now, they just wanted time on their own, to sit quietly with her, to try and come to terms with what had occurred, to reflect. At least, after what she had suffered for so many years, she was free of her illness; at peace. Perhaps some consolation for what her parents were now enduring themselves.

The trauma of attending church on the Sunday was a step too far. Being surrounded by people who meant well but whose expressions of sympathy would certainly have produced floods of tears - and not just from Sue and Nick - was not an experience they wished to undertake. After all, they were facing enough of an ordeal in church on Tuesday at the funeral.

"We would not have been able to control our emotions," suggested Nick. "The adapted vehicle we had for Rebecca had not been used since the Saturday when we had returned from Wales and the battery had drained. So we called out the RAC and then decided to give it a run down the motorway towards Warrington. We ended up going into a garden centre. It seemed a daft thing to do, but we wandered round in a daze, and then we called on Sue's brother and his wife. We had a coffee with them and then returned home."

A visitor that afternoon was an inquisitive young friend of Rebecca's. Alex, 13, was one of many children who were encountering death for the first time, and wanted to know what happens when someone dies. "There were a lot of questions, innocent and well meant," Nick continued. "In their own way his questions brought us quite a lot of comfort, and he wanted to know what time he should leave school for the funeral and what he should wear."

Like Alex, so many had been touched by the happiness she had brought; so many stunned by her death. As her carer, Jane Young had been a constant companion. She had rushed home from holiday to be at her bedside the day before she died and was one of several who called at the chapel to say her goodbyes.

"She looked lovely and Barney was there with her," said Jane. "I was in there half an hour and a lady popped her head in and asked if I was all right. She went out and every time I went to go I couldn't do it, and turned round and found something else to say. While I was there I placed two sweets, Lovehearts, into her right hand. One said 'Sweet Dreams', the other

'My Friend'. I will always remember the 'I love yous', the hugs and kisses. Although she was a very friendly child, she chose her friends. She chose you to be her friend."

Inevitably, thoughts about the funeral were never far from the couple's minds. Most of the arrangements were complete but there were other things, trivial in the bigger picture, that nevertheless required attention.

"We had to arrange for refreshments after the funeral," said Nick, "and also for family and friends who were travelling from various parts of the country and who needed something before the funeral, which wasn't until 2.30pm. They were things to think about that you didn't want to think about, but which you had to focus on.

"Many people had been in touch. It was something to hang your hat on when things were so desperate. What also amazed us was that we got bundles of cards. There was a steady trickle for a day or two but after that we were absolutely inundated to the extent that the postman was putting all the cards in bundles and delivering them that way. On one day we had two bundles delivered, probably 100 cards from all sorts of people who had been there at some time of Rebecca's life. There were many messages from people of different religions, too. In all, we received over 400 cards and messages of sympathy.

"Another person who turned up was our social worker at the time we were making our application for adoption, and then when Rebecca had been placed with us. She had moved on to another section of the Adoption Service but she had heard about Rebecca's passing and wanted to see us."

One of the couple's biggest worries was whether everyone who had known Rebecca and wished to attend the funeral were aware of when it was taking place. They need not have worried. If people didn't know before, they were able to read a story about her in the Liverpool Echo on the Monday night. She had been the subject of several news stories during her life, concerning her illness, her 'Make A Wish' trip and her athletics successes, and the paper used one of the many photographs they had of her in reporting her passing.

Sue and Nick finalised plans for the service. "David had very kindly offered to do a eulogy and we had asked others to do readings," said Nick.

"I had decided that I wanted to say something because I thought it was right. I wanted to speak about Rebecca's life and I spent a lot of time trying to put that together."

Tuesday, the day of the funeral, was designed to be a celebration of Rebecca's life. Given everything that had happened to her in those 13 years it had been a remarkable one. And, yes, it was going to be traumatic for her parents, but a comfort to them were the many happy memories of their daughter, a truly exceptional young lady, to surround them.

"We just knew it was a day that had to be got through," Sue reflected. "We didn't want to do it because it was a case of making things even more final than they already were. We knew people were travelling from around the country to be with us to support us and family and friends would be at the church. We had to do it and didn't want to let Rebecca down. We just got up and started to pull ourselves together. We had slept but the quality wasn't there.

"We hoped the service would be how we wanted it to be and how we thought Rebecca would like it. We went to the funeral parlour just to say private goodbyes and talk to Rebecca one last time. We couldn't stay as long as we wanted to because we were thinking people would be turning up and there was no-one at home to let them in."

They had received a card that morning from Childwall Church. It was especially for bereaved families for the day of a funeral and contained prayers and prose.

"It captured the way we were feeling, and we were very touched by it," Nick observed. "We were numbed but feeling a bit worked up as to whether everything would go right. People started arriving and, as ever on these occasions, they were chatting away but you just felt you were on the outside of the conversations.

"Then came the ring on the doorbell and everyone hushed. It hits you seeing the cortege and realising what was about to unfold. When we arrived at the crossroads where the church was it was crowded with cars. I don't suppose it hit us immediately that they were there for Rebecca's funeral. I remember the minister met us and he said there were quite a few people in church. There were people waiting outside, including Rebecca's taxi driver. It was his way of paying his respects. In church, I saw a reflection through the glass window of lots of people, many of whom were standing, which was quite amazing."

The sight that greeted them as they walked into church took their breath away. "We both stopped because we were so taken aback by how full the church was," said Sue. "I hadn't seen it that full for a long time. It was pretty full for Rebecca's christening because people had to sit in the side pews, but for the church to be so full that people were standing two or three deep was amazing. The thought that all these people had come because they had some sort of connection, predominantly with Rebecca, helped to carry me through the next couple of hours."

The congregation included many youngsters - Rebecca's friends at Childwall and church. During the service John and Barbara read bible passages and David, as he began his eulogy, looked out at the vast numbers and said "Wow!"

Said Nick: "It encapsulated our feelings about the number of people who were supporting us in church. I remember going out to say my bit and do my best to keep it together because Rebecca didn't like to see us or anyone else upset. I remember thanking so many people that had helped her in so many ways - hospitals, schools, church, Claire House, her personal friends and family, and I tried to include a few memories that might raise a smile. I held it together just. Then I was conscious of people clapping."

The ordeal wasn't quite over, but at least there was a light-hearted moment that lifted spirits as the cortege left for the journey to Springwood Crematorium.

"The majority of people held it together until Nick said the last few words and then the tears started to flow," said Sue. "Going in to church everyone is facing the front, but going out all eyes seemed to be on you, and I just wanted to get out as quickly as possible. We were very surprised that the hearse and funeral cars were in the car park because the way the church was situated it didn't lend itself to large cars turning round in the car park. We didn't think too much of it until we got into the funeral car. I just thought they would reverse out but the funeral director marched out of the gates that led directly onto the junction and just held up the traffic for Rebecca to drive out through a 'no entry' sign to the other side of the junction. It lifted the moment and it was right that she held up the traffic!"

The church hall had been chosen as the perfect venue for the reception. Rebecca loved the church and had so many good times there. But it was packed and when Sue, Nick, family members and friends returned, they could hardly get into the room. The warmth which enveloped them as they talked to everyone gave them the incentive to cope with the situation. And they were comforted, too, by the comments written by so many in a commemorative book which people were asked to sign. A few tears were shed as they read them later.

Nick had been given as much time off work as he wanted. The following few days after the funeral were no easier than the ones that had gone before. In fact, life was never going to be the same again for them. Friends were very kind. They appreciated the invitations for meals because being at home without their daughter was too hard to bear.

They were kept busy responding to the hundreds of cards they had received. They also faced a dilemma. A holiday had been booked with Jennie and David to Majorca. Of course, Rebecca had been due to go with them. It was only a fortnight away. In the past few weeks it had been well down the list of priorities. Now, it was decision time.

Nick felt that in the circumstances a break might do them good. "I said I would go back to work on the Monday and then two weeks later we would go on holiday. We just didn't want to be at home because it was very empty. While we were away Dave Jones, an electrician friend, was extremely kind and arranged for the lift to be taken out of Rebecca's bedroom and the ceiling re-plastered.

"The holiday allowed a period of time to reflect and think over what had gone on and people's kindnesses. But it was also a very odd feeling because we had never gone away without her. There were times when we were very emotional. We went away the weekend after we got back, too. We were seeing friends and stayed in a small country hotel. Sitting down at breakfast, the two of us looking at each other, we just felt completely and utterly lost."

With her husband's return to work, Sue ensured she had plenty to occupy her mind, especially if she was at home. But, again, friends came to the rescue.

"Whether someone had an invisible rota going for the first few weeks I am not sure. I don't think I did have much time by myself because I went for that many cups of coffee. When there wasn't anyone about I didn't want to be in the house so I walked and walked. Anywhere. Probably places where I knew I wouldn't meet people. When Nick came in in the evening during the two weeks before the holiday we just pounded the streets, just talking.

"We talked to express our feelings. Some nights it was helpful. Some nights it was not. It was awful because of what had happened just trying to grasp the enormity of it - the feeling of being alone, not really alone, but lonely. Bereft.

She added: "We went away for a couple more weekends but it didn't make any difference. We had good times while we were there, but it was always the coming back. There is always the coming back feeling - the coming back to what seemed a very empty house. It doesn't matter how often we go away it's still the coming back that hurts."

Chapter Fifteen

A Special Bond

A MOTHER'S love is considered to be one of the greatest gifts.

From the moment a baby is born a special bond is created between parent and child.

Rebecca was six months old when she became Sue's little girl. But that was never a disadvantage because the relationship between the two became so strong in such a short period of time. And the love she and Nick bestowed on their daughter was inestimable.

They may have considered themselves lucky to have adopted such a beautiful baby, but equally, Rebecca was fortunate to have such wonderful parents.

Jacqui Brearley, Nick's sister, saw at close quarters the impact Rebecca's arrival had on the couple and what a wonderful life she was given.

"When Rebecca came along we were so thrilled for them," she said. "They so deserved her. She was very special to us all. We loved her to bits. At the time, we didn't have children and I felt she was a gift from God for all of us. She was fantastic right through her life.

"When it became apparent that she was poorly it came as a terrible shock. It's at times like that when you wished you didn't live as far away, but being in High Wycombe meant it wasn't easy to be around. We tried to visit as often as we could.

"There was that awful period when nobody knew what was happening, but Nick and Sue have always been incredibly brave, incredibly strong, wonderful parents. I am firmly convinced that it was God's plan that they should be her parents and she could not have had better parents. They have shown tremendous courage with what they have had to cope with.

"Sue, particularly, has probably borne the brunt of the workload and stress and strain of being Rebecca's carer. But she always had a sense of humour throughout it all. She engrossed herself in activities with Rebecca and kept her active, doing athletics, and she was so proud of the medals she won. That was partly down to Sue and her hard work and determination to give her that happy, normal experience. I think she is marvellous. She just adapted as the goalposts were constantly moving for both of them. Rebecca's needs were changing and she had periods when she was very ill and the pressure on both of them was intense, but Sue coped with it. They were testing times. It's only when these things come along that you realise how much strength you have inside and Sue and Nick had incredible strength, as Rebecca had as well. At church, Sue helped to run the children's club Rebecca went to, and she got Rebecca involved in cooking and other things she loved to do. So Rebecca had a lot of wonderful experiences she wouldn't have had if she hadn't had Sue and Nick as her parents.

"She was always a beautiful child. We have such happy memories of times we spent with them. When she was a toddler we went to Cornwall and we were on a beach having such fun playing, paddling and digging in the sand, and she would be climbing all over John. She was such a delightful little girl.

"Her smile had a particular power because you felt that the sun had come out and was warming the whole of your body. Her face glowed and it made the hairs on the back of your neck stand on end. Considering what she went through she had such courage and determination. You could see the love between her and Sue and Nick. It was fabulous and a lesson to us all."

News of Rebecca's illness stunned Jacqui and her family and their hearts went out to Sue and Nick.

"I felt they were being tortured," she said. "It was awful. She went downhill slowly. I was so shocked when I first saw her connected up to the respirator. It was heartbreaking. I felt angry for Sue and Nick and angry with God. How could He let this happen? Such a special child, a gift, and it got me so frustrated, which probably wasn't the right way of dealing with it.

"Rebecca was on the prayer list at our church, and had been for many years right through to the end. I know my faith is patchy, not what it should be, but I do believe in the power of prayer and I hoped they felt supported by that. I know everyone at Allerton URC were praying for them. I think Sue thought they were on every prayer list in Liverpool, as you would have wanted them to be, but they must have felt frustration and anger. It was desperately sad.

"I don't think even if you can face the truth of a situation that you really do appreciate how bad things are until they start deteriorating. It's always when things start to go wrong that you really appreciate what a gift life and health is and that we are all so fortunate. My impression of them was that they felt every single moment with Rebecca was precious and I believe because of that the quality of the life they had together over those 13 years was deeper, stronger and more special than a lot of children never have in a lifetime."

Jacqui and John now have two children of their own, Matthew and Lydia. As they grew up they built up a friendship with Rebecca that was always special and they enjoyed so many wonderful times together.

"Matthew loved Rebecca dearly. He and Lydia both talk about her. When she was four, I remember Rebecca was sitting on a mat on the floor in hospital with all the tubes connected to the machines. She was getting better and stronger and Matthew was crawling round her and they were having a game.

"Matthew remembered Rebecca coming to Lydia's baptism and being part of that service. That was very special for us," went on Jacqui. "She lit the candle and put the sign of the cross on Lydia's forehead and so did Matthew. Lydia always had lovely cuddles with Rebecca and she knew about her love of Barney because she always talked about her purple cuddly toy. They would often play one of their favourite games - hide and seek - and when we went out anywhere Matthew wanted to push Rebecca in her wheelchair.

"When we went to the park it must have been hard for Sue and Nick. Rebecca couldn't go into the playground and play like the other kids, but we would walk round, play ball and throw it to her. Sometimes when she came to our house she would bring her bouncy castle. That was lovely and the children enjoyed that. She also had a little kitchen which they had fun with and Matthew and Rebecca played bean bag games. They understood that when they played with Rebecca it was trying to do things she could do. We achieved that to a certain level, although there may have been times when we should have done it more."

It is difficult for children to understand why someone should spend so long in hospital and even harder to appreciate the extent of their illness. But when that youngster whom they have loved dies the explanations become almost impossible. The families were close, they were together for the weekend break in Wales that was cut short when Rebecca was rushed home, and they shared, with other family members, the anguish of Rebecca's death.

"Rebecca, Matthew and Lydia had a special bond," Jacqui continued. "He knew Rebecca was ill and we told him how poorly she was. Children always ask questions and he wanted to understand what was happening with her tracheostomy and why she needed suction. Even though we tried to explain to him how serious she was I think it was a big shock to him when Rebecca died. He was devastated. He still misses her, as we all do, but children have a way of handling it."

She expressed tremendous admiration for her brother and sister-in-law in the dignified way they have dealt with their loss, and pointed to the strength of a marriage that has remained rock-like during their years of caring and the suffering they have encountered. "I so admire them for the way they have handled everything, and now the way they are coping with the grief of losing their daughter.

"There are people you hear about tragically who don't stay together after they have lost a child. But I believe if the foundations of a relationship are right it binds you together like super glue. They have always been a happy couple, but obviously weren't happy when they were going through this terrible tragedy. But, as a couple, their relationship is probably stronger as a result.

"Although it must be awful at times, they have coped so well in the positive way they have approached life after Rebecca. Sue, particularly, has picked herself up. She is very strong, talented, marvellous. She has gone on cake decorating courses and has shown she is an enthusiastic person who succeeds in whatever she turns her hands to. They deserve as much happiness as they can get.

"You try to see things from their perspective and feel the pain they are going through and try to ease it. I feel we are very close. Matthew and Lydia love them so much and they are a wonderful auntie and uncle. It doesn't make things better from the point of view that they have lost Rebecca, but I hope they feel that they have the love of Matthew and Lydia, who will have so many memories of Rebecca for the whole of their lives. She was a wonderful cousin to them. We all miss her terribly. I believe that Rebecca lives on in us all with the joy she gave to everyone. She lives on in Matthew and Lydia because of what they shared in a beautiful friendship and the times they had together."

Having experienced the fragility of life, particularly in a young life within the family, Jacqui looks at her own children in a more discerning way. She realises that having a child is an incredible privilege and the opportunity presents itself to treasure every moment.

"Nobody knows what's round the corner. You have to go for it, work hard, and make the most of the time you have with your kids. I know I am not sometimes as patient as I should be with Lydia, because she can be a bit of a handful, but it does make me aware, having seen what Sue and Nick have been through, how things that are so precious can be taken away. There are times when you might be tired and you don't feel you should be giving them the time you do, but Sue worked so hard and was always there. Even if she had been up all night and lost several nights' sleep in a row, she never stopped. When Rebecca was in hospital for long periods, she would have been with her until she went to sleep, and then returned when she was waking up. She couldn't have had a more devoted mother. It does make you realise how time is precious; how your children are precious."

Sue, who retained close ties with Childwall C of E School once Rebecca had left, has been working there part-time in the office. Nick also has links there, being on the board of governors and as a trustee.

One of the main features at the school is a special garden constructed as a permanent memorial for what Rebecca meant to the staff and pupils. Her parents, family members and school representatives, attended an official opening.

"It is a lovely place where staff or pupils can go and sit if they want somewhere quiet," said head Diane Shaw. "I had always wanted a sensory garden and I knew Rebecca's sense of smell and touch were things we could key into, so we created it for her and it was opened last year.

"The staff were so upset when we heard the news about Rebecca. We had a special service in school on the day. We lit a candle and we had prayers and we asked for people to share memories, which they did. It was mainly the staff by then because it was two years since she had left, but many children still remembered her. We had her photograph on the screen and we cried together, and I always think it is important that children need to see it is all right to cry. You get strength from that and also strength from the fact everyone is praying for you and everyone else.

"I have so much respect for Sue and Nick and I am delighted Sue is back here working with us. She has become invaluable."

Sandfield head John Hudson related a touching moment after the school had held their service in Rebecca's memory. "One of the young people in the athletics team with her told me how sad it was about Rebecca and how she was his friend and he would never forget her. I told him we would always remember her. She was always very much part of the spirit of the team."

Sue Barry, PE co-ordinator, added: "Dan was on the ramp ball event and bean bag target event with her and what he said after she died was very touching. The year after Rebecca died and we were back with the athletics again another pupil, Gerard, was on the team bus when we were coming back on the Saturday night from the two-day event. We were in first place, and he said 'let's win it tomorrow for Rebecca'. He said it without prompting and I thought it said it all for the team.

"She had a great attitude of having a go at anything and not letting anything get in the way," added Sue. "That's very much a part of the school and that is a great push for independence. Her laugh was infectious and she loved singing and bouncing up and down in the wheelchair to the music."

In his tribute, Mr Hudson said: "She was a lovely pupil to have within the school and a model to others in her determination, and a tribute to her family as well. You could go two ways - totally wrap her in cotton wool and keep all danger away or you could go for it. And her life was very much 'go for it' and that came out. It was Sue and Nick's attitude and it was also Rebecca's. That enriched her life and everyone around her."

Chapter Sixteen

My Special Friend

NOTHING compares with the wonder of watching a child growing up.

As a baby, there is the fragility and the helplessness; the need to rely on others for existence. As they get older and start walking and talking they benefit from the guidance of parents and close family, their learning processes begin and their personality gradually takes shape. The formative years are important in determining their potential. Independence and education play their part in progress, and their developing characteristics can influence what the future may hold.

But one factor so intrinsic to family life that cannot be underestimated is the bond between parents and child, based on the most potent feeling of all - love.

Rebecca's start in life had been uncertain. As a baby she initially needed a foster mum, but it was almost as if fate, that strange phenomena, stepped in when Sue and Nick entered her life. Here was a couple who yearned for a child of their own, were desperate to enjoy the experience of parenthood, and could offer her love in abundance. It was almost as if they were made for each other and from that point the six month old bundle of joy became the central figure of one extremely happy family.

It seemed that her fortunes had changed; her unhappy start to life had been put behind her. Yet later came another cruel twist when Rebecca was struck down with her illness. All seemed lost. But it wasn't. What hadn't been taken into account was the youngster's undoubted courage and Sue and Nick's rock-like strength, offering support and love to their daughter. But there were so many more of us as back-up to her parents, adding our support, love and encouragement in her ups and downs.

Her life may only have lasted 13 years, but what a fulfilling life it was, full of accomplishment, happiness, enrichment, innocence, laughter, determination and spirit. Oh, yes, most definitely spirit!

I took great pleasure in seeing that young life develop; delighted to have had a small part to play in it.

From the moment I saw her being carried through the doors of Allerton United Reformed Church on that first occasion it was obvious what she meant to Sue and Nick. Through their personal circumstances she was a special gift, but it was only as the years unfolded and her illness had such a dramatic effect that we all realised just how special Rebecca was.

Jennie and I are close friends of Sue and Nick and we, along with so many others, were thrilled for them as they revealed the new addition to the family.

We enjoyed the many opportunities we had to be with Rebecca, whether babysitting, at family gatherings or church functions. She loved stories and I remember occasions as she grew up - still a slender, delicate little girl - sitting on my knee listening intently to tales from her favourite books.

Rebecca never felt uneasy in the company of adults and quite quickly she and I struck up a lovely rapport. As she started talking it became a source of amusement that for a time she was unable to pronounce the word 'uncle', so I literally became her 'Auntie David'! I didn't mind. She would giggle almost every time she said it, as if it were our little joke, and I felt it somehow cemented our friendship.

But there were other times it was a joy to be with her, on outings or holidays, and wherever we were there was always that sense of fun, sometimes in a mischievous way, that underlined her love for living.

On one occasion when we went strawberry picking I noticed she was selecting the un-ripened or bad ones, so I showed her how to throw them away. Next thing I knew, she was picking some of the farmer's best and throwing them away, too.

Our antics occasionally caused embarrassment for her mum and dad. But we didn't care! There was the incident on a visit to the beach at Portmadoc when Rebecca and I marched up and down like soldiers with buckets on our head in front of other holidaymakers; there were the silly games we played; our ability to make a show of ourselves on the dance floor. It was all about having a good time - and we always did - and usually Rebecca would be sporting a huge grin.

She would sometimes point to her golden locks, informing me that I had very little hair. So, after initially looking hurt, I would drape some of her hair over my head, always creating the response, 'you are so silly,' followed by peels of laughter.

There were the lovely holidays our families shared together, with Rebecca always the life and soul of the party, whether playing on the sands, enjoying the hotel's food or boogying at the children's disco.

Jennie and I felt proud to be asked by her mum and dad to become her godparents. She meant so much to us.

Not surprisingly, she touched so many hearts with her spellbinding smile, bubbly personality, and happy-go-lucky attitude that cascaded down on people like spray from a champagne bottle. In fact, one of my business friends was so captivated by Rebecca's passion for life when we met during a new year's eve party in the Lake District that he invited her and her parents to his cricket club's presentation evening. That was one example of the effect she had.

As restrictive as her sickness became, Rebecca remained a shining example of what could be achieved. She may have been vulnerable with her life so often balanced on a knife-edge, but she was tough, too, her bravery and resilience in the face of adversity shining through; defying doctors and their predictions, and always maintaining a fighting spirit.

She accompanied her mum and me on many Wirral Coastal Charity Walks in aid of Claire House, prepared to be pushed in her wheelchair for much of the 15 miles each year, irrespective of the weather conditions. They generally provided little in the way of incident, but I remember feeling extremely worried on one occasion a few years ago. It was my turn to push Rebecca but we had reached a part of the course where we had to pull her up an incline covered in deep, fine sand. Unfortunately, I misjudged a difficult section and the wheelchair, complete with Rebecca, tipped over to one side, spilling her out of the chair onto the sand. Luckily, she was not injured and once we had put the chair upright and brushed the sand off her, she was soon sitting comfortably again. But I continued apologising to her right to the finish!

Her illness was devastating, her subsequent death at such a tender age heartbreaking. But her life was one of astounding fulfilment, thanks to the devotion of her wonderful parents.

She had an aura about her, her captivating beauty and wonderful smile, just a part of a huge personality.

Rebecca was an inspiration. You could never feel downhearted in her presence, even when you knew her illness was having an effect, because she would not allow it to overwhelm her.

As devastating as it was when she died, her legacy of love, warmth, zest and spirit will live on. She has left behind so many wonderful memories and I wanted to write this book as a tribute to her extraordinary life, revealing her exceptional courage in the face of illness, but also to capture the many magical highlights she experienced.

To me, Rebecca wasn't a child. She was a special friend.

We will all miss her. But we will never forget her.

Chapter Seventeen

Always In Our Thoughts

TIME

In our day to day life people say
"You cope so well."
If only they knew.
You feel like a swan gliding along
Whilst inside you are struggling to stay afloat

But the snapshots in your mind of the happy times,
the smiles, laughter, the memories, keep you going.

You taught us how to look at the world through your eyes,
To take things at a slower pace,
Watch the clouds pass by,
Enjoy the sun rise and set.
You taught us to enjoy the simple things of life,
To appreciate the small milestones as well as the big.
But, most of all, not to judge.

Time marches on
But in our hearts it stands still
The world carries on
But in our hearts it stands still.
Life goes on,
Although you are gone.
In our hearts you live on.
- SUE PYE

TIME, according to the famous quotation, is a great healer.

But no amount of time can heal the heartache of losing a loved one, especially your only child.

It is two years since Sue and Nick Pye said farewell to their daughter, but in the time that has elapsed since that July day in 2008 life has not been the same for them - and never will.

Rebecca was the centre of their world, a cherished gift who brought so much happiness to family life.

They accept they will never overcome the distress and torment of her death, only that the many treasured memories they shared together will provide adequate comfort. Their love for her overflowed, both in the good times and bad, and when she was cruelly struck down by illness that love acted as an antidote and strength during her brave battle.

Henry Jackson van Dyke, an American author, educator and clergyman born in the 19th century, once wrote: 'Time is too slow for those who wait, too swift for those who fear, too long for those who grieve, too short for those who rejoice, but for those who love, time is eternity'.

For Sue and Nick their grief is on-going, but their love for her remains indestructible. In day-to-day life they put on a brave face, not betraying their inner feelings, but the pain is always with them.

"I read somewhere which is very apt that people like us get up each day and put a mask on," stated Sue. "However you are feeling you put this mask on, go out and greet the world and pretend to act normally. Some days it's a lot easier than others but you try not to let the mask slip in public. It's very different when you are at home because the mask can be taken off and you can have your thoughts behind closed doors.

"People give you a certain amount of time when they think you should be over something, so it's easier to put that mask on and let them think you are coping."

The couple are comforted by the continued support of family and friends and during the past couple of years both have immersed themselves in work and various activities. But everything they do, wherever they go, they suffer tinges of guilt that they shouldn't be enjoying themselves because Rebecca is no longer with them.

Nick alluded to the fact that both he and his wife experience dark days and, when faced with additional complications that life has a habit of throwing at you, those dark days become darker.

"I was told that as time goes on you would be able to laugh about some of the good times you had as well as cry about the sad times. That's probably true because you do remember the happy things, and often things we do remind us of the times we enjoyed with Rebecca. So, yes, we can smile.

"It was easier for me when I went back to work. After Rebecca died it was possible to get engrossed in work and the sad events wouldn't cross my mind for an hour or so, and then I would feel terribly guilty that thoughts of Rebecca hadn't entered my head. But other times when I have been driving to work or coming home there might be a tune on the radio that signified a specific time in her life so it brought memories flooding back.

"The void, however, is huge. Very nice things have happened in our lives since but not as nice as they might have been if Rebecca had still been about. You cope because what else can you do. Sometimes there are days when you don't want to face the world but you need to carry on and try to be positive. She's never more than a thought away, but life will never be the same."

For so long, Sue's days had been demanding looking after Rebecca's every need. She was used to being on call twenty four seven. But in the aftermath of her daughter's passing she found herself suddenly thrust into a totally alien environment where there was little to do, hours dragged and her mission in life had been destroyed.

"There was just an emptiness," she admitted. "I was wondering how to fill so many hours. As weeks and months went by I found things to do, going to work for a few hours a week and taking up cake decorating, which I do enjoy, but I still wish I didn't have the time to do it."

Their spirits have been lifted through an awareness of Rebecca's presence on certain occasions and the positive effect it has had on them. During times of bereavement at Claire House the Butterfly Suite is used for distraught parents and Sue and Nick adopted the symbol of the butterfly, given that its short, very fragile, but beautiful life had many parallels to that of Rebecca's.

Said Sue: "If we are feeling down we might walk past a shop window and coincidentally there might be an ornament of a butterfly there. So you think that Rebecca is looking after us.

"Recently, I was getting ready to go to work on one of those 'I really don't want to go to work' days. I wondered whether I should ring up and tell them I wasn't well. But I looked up and just by the window was a butterfly and I said 'okay, Rebecca, I am going', and went off to work. So she isn't far away. She seems to make her presence felt.

"It's very strange, comforting, yet it is also still very sad because you wish you weren't seeing butterflies and thinking that way because she should still be with us. But she isn't and that's how we know that spiritually - not a word I use a lot - she is still around us."

A touching occasion when the couple were visiting friends at a farm in Worcestershire was indicative of that presence and how a butterfly once again played a symbolic part. It occurred 12 months after Rebecca died when the friends decided to set aside part of a field in a beautiful location with amazing views as a little remembrance garden for their family.

"They wanted to plant a tree for Rebecca and wild flowers as a lasting tribute because she was so well loved by them and their wider family," Nick recalled. "They asked us if we would like to join them and help with the planting. The weather hadn't been particularly good, but then the sun came out as we walked to the field. Someone suggested that a little reading and meditation would be appropriate so Sue read out a verse about a butterfly the children at Childwall Primary had used in the ceremony at the sensory garden. We had earlier mentioned to our friends about how butterflies were significant to us.

"Just as she was reading the verse what should happen but a butterfly came down. It wasn't just noticed by us but also by our friends, and they were really taken by it and said how amazing it was that the butterfly should choose that time to fly close by. So it has been a symbol of Rebecca being about, and with us, no matter where we are."

Rebecca's love for life was always apparent and her happy disposition rubbed off on everyone she met. She wanted them to feel as she did, and would even tell her mum and dad off if they had a difference of opinion.

One of her gifts to them had been a calendar from school which read: 'To Mum and Dad, be happy every day and always. Love Rebecca'. It epitomised the way she wanted to be and how she perceived others to be. Her parents, though, find it extremely difficult at times.

"We try," Sue admitted. "We try to be what we were to her while she was living. We try to be positive. It's not easy, most definitely not. You can feel guilty about being happy. That's the last thing she would have wanted, but sometimes you can't help it. There have been numerous times when we have returned home after having an enjoyable time out and both of us have said we shouldn't have been there or done that because Rebecca should have been with us. You can't help but feel empty even though you have your happy moments. Emptiness is at the bottom of it all."

They agree to a feeling of incompleteness now Rebecca is no longer around, but concede there is nothing they can do about it.

"It is like when Rebecca came to us we were completing a jigsaw," Sue continued. "Now she has gone that piece of the jigsaw is missing, like a piece out of our heart, and it is never going to be replaced. It has disappeared forever."

The impact she had on young and old was mesmeric. Some people did not necessarily have a close bond with her, but during the past two years many of them have told Sue and Nick of experiences that have prompted recollections of times when they met Rebecca. It might have been through the positive way she approached life, even when she was restricted by illness, the happiness she exuded, the radiant smile or the sparkle in her eye. But there is no doubt her personality had a remarkable effect on so many.

One of them, Rebecca's young friend Alex, still visits to chat to her parents about her, reflecting how she touched the hearts of young and old alike.

Nick said: "We are helped by people's concern all the time and Alex often comes round. Perhaps it is his way of overcoming what he found was very traumatic with Rebecca dying. It is lovely that he has kept in touch, but so have Rebecca's friends from church. They have met twice on the anniversaries of Rebecca's death just to sit and talk and remember her and we find that very touching.

"It is obvious she is still in the thoughts of Rebecca's cousins, Matthew and Lydia. She is only five and asked us recently where Rebecca had gone because she missed her. We told her simply that Rebecca had gone to live with Jesus.

"So many have something to remember her by. There are church friends who remind us often of times when events were taking place there and they would be in the kitchen making toast and tea. One of them, Denise, always tells the story that whenever the smell of toast permeated down the corridor Rebecca would leave whatever she was doing and go straight to the kitchen to see if she could get something to eat before anyone else - with the usual grin on her face. She would hang back afterwards to see if she could help in the kitchen in the hope of getting something else. These are memories from other people that we can smile about."

Despite her short life her parents are thankful for so many wonderful memories, but of course there is the regret that there will be no more.

"We can't make any more of those memories," her mum said, sadly. "We have only got the ones we have to reflect on, whereas with most families you create more memories as the children grow up. As Nick said when he spoke at the funeral: 'Oh, but for a while longer'."

The opportunity of watching their daughter grow up into a young woman has been denied them and there is no consolation, just a sense of sadness of what might have been.

"We are very grateful for what we had," said her dad. "In fact, we had a great deal longer time with Rebecca than we were led to believe we might have, but it is human nature that however long you have, and however good that time was, you still want more.

"Rebecca's fighting qualities were such that you never quite thought that ultimately she would succumb to the illness. You always thought she would keep on going. But it wasn't to be. We have had some lovely times in the last couple of years, but it doesn't feel right because Rebecca has not been there to share them with us."

The family's generosity has seen others benefit as a result of monetary gifts Rebecca had received down the years but hadn't spent. Two of the beneficiaries were her schools - Childwall C of E, who built a sensory garden in her memory, and Sandfield Park, who bought a silver trophy and engraved it as the 'Rebecca Pye Sports Day Cup'. Her parents felt the remainder of the money should go to Claire House.

Sue explained: "They had been so supportive of us all so I spoke to Karen Roberts, head of care. We knew that the hospice was always desperate for funds for every day running costs and we felt that monies donated by people after the funeral should go into that fund. We thought the money that belonged to Rebecca should be used in a practical way to benefit Claire House and also act as a lasting memory of Rebecca.

"They had recently had a conservatory donated to them. They were grateful for that, but it was just a shell, without flooring or furniture, so we said we would like to furnish it. We were quite happy just to hand over the money for them to do it, but they asked me if I would like to go out and buy the items. It took me a while to get round to doing it because it never felt like the right time, but I had everything delivered to the hospice, set the room up and didn't let anyone in until it was completed. The staff were delighted with it.

"The room isn't actually for the children. We felt it should be used by parents or staff who might need a short break, or so parents had somewhere to go in the event of a bereavement. So it is a practical room, a light and bright room, and I think Rebecca would be pleased that it is there."

But her memory won't just live on in Claire House. It will live on in Alder Hey Children's Hospital as doctors and nurses remember that brave little battler who refused to give in to Leigh Syndrome; in her schools, with the many friends she made; at Allerton United Reformed Church, where she was loved from the time she first appeared as a six month old baby; by her grandparents, other family members and friends.

And, of course, at her loving family home, blessed with devoted parents who treasured every living moment of her short but fulfilling life.

"Rebecca had so many qualities," said her dad. "She was happy, spirited, mischievous, and always tried her best. She showed tremendous affection for all those around her, had a great zest for life and living to its fullest extent, no matter what difficulties lay in her way."

And her mum's lasting memories were of her physical qualities - her hugs, her smile and her laughter.

"She would always have a hug and a kiss," added Sue. "When Nick came home I would give him a kiss and she didn't want to be left out. So we would kneel down to the wheelchair and we would have group hugs, and she always gave a great big bear hug. She was also a people person. When we had family occasions she was always sad to see people going."

Sue and Nick will be forever grateful for those precious years they had as Rebecca's parents, and grateful, too, to be blessed with such a beautiful daughter and the unbridled happiness that family life brought. It is an experience they will never forget, and they commend adoption to anyone who might be considering it.

For them, Rebecca was a truly wonderful gift!

REBECCA

Soft skin and silky hair
Your hugs and smiles
Those dancing eyes
The mischief that lay behind them.

To bottle that smile
Oh, to bottle that smile
Would have brought joy to millions.
It warmed my heart in the bleakest times
Just that simple smile.

If only that smile was in a bottle
I could open it a little every day
Enjoy the warmth it gave
But then it might fade away.
I will just keep it in my heart
Forever where you will stay.
- SUE PYE

171

About the Author

David Jones is a Liverpool-born journalist of over 40 years. Most of that time was spent working on the *Liverpool Echo* in the Sports Department. He was Sports Editor for eight years and wrote the book *Liverpool Football Club – A History* in 1989. He was so inspired by the bravery and determination of his goddaughter, Rebecca, despite her serious illness, that he wrote this book in her memory.

Lightning Source UK Ltd.
Milton Keynes UK
16 March 2011

169313UK00002B/11/P